lonely planet

ARUBA,

Bailey Freeman, Robert Isenberg

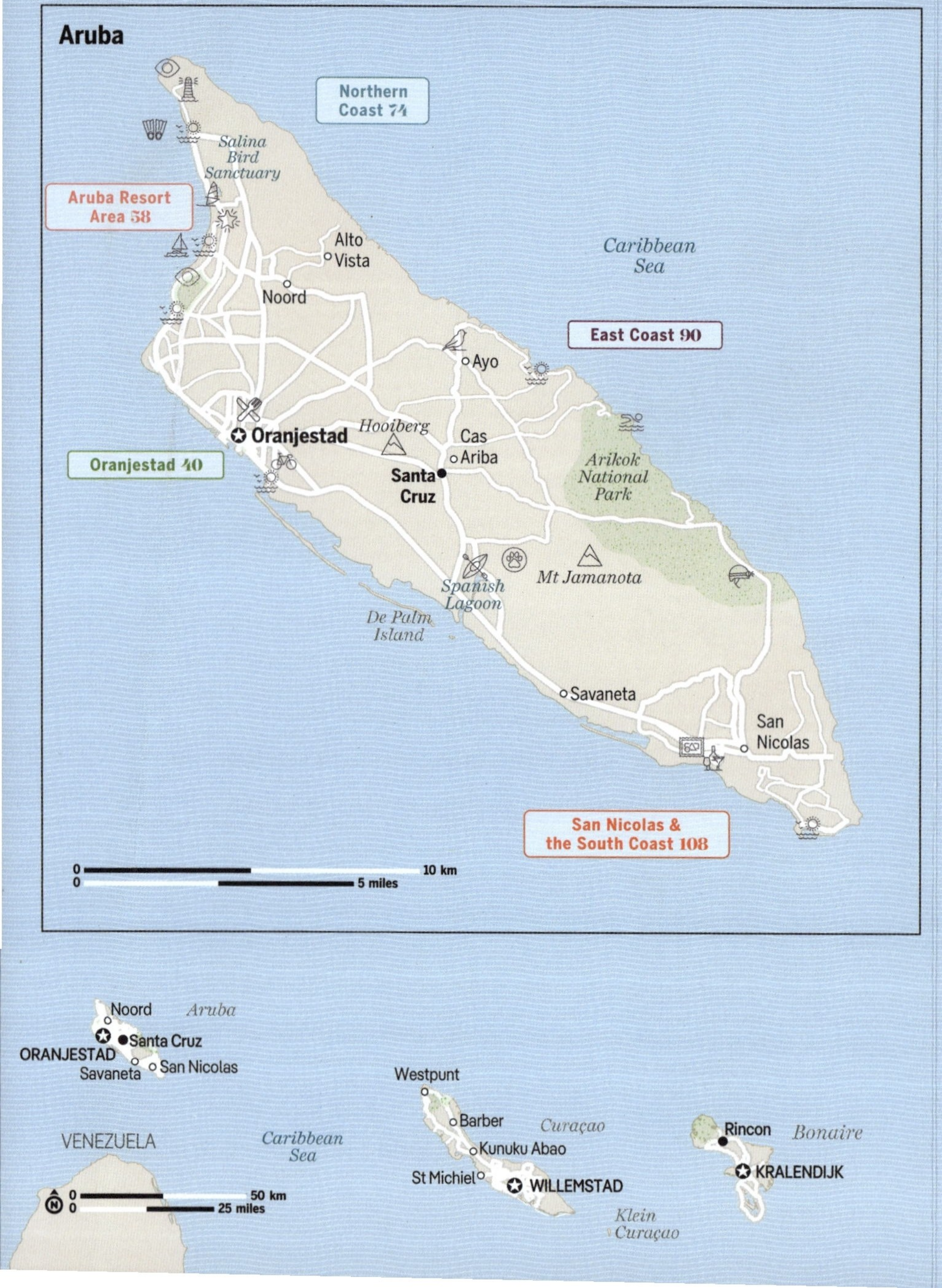

Aruba

Northern Coast 74

Salina Bird Sanctuary

Aruba Resort Area 58

Alto Vista

Noord

Caribbean Sea

East Coast 90

Ayo

Oranjestad

Hooiberg

Cas Ariba

Santa Cruz

Oranjestad 40

Arikok National Park

Mt Jamanota

Spanish Lagoon

De Palm Island

Savaneta

San Nicolas

San Nicolas & the South Coast 108

0 — 10 km
0 — 5 miles

Coral reef (p158), Bonaire

Contents

GANZ TWINS/SHUTTERSTOCK

Above Beach, Bonaire (p128)

Palm Beach

Aruba's most convivial seafront

Palm Beach is the kingpin of Aruba's resort beaches. Ivory-white sands and swaying palm trees stretch down its 3.2km length, and international travelers and locals alike bask in the coastal beauty here by the thousands.

16 minutes from central Oranjestad

▶ p65

Aruba's Eagle Beach

Pristine sand and sea breeze

Eagle Beach's world-renowned reputation is merited – this wide beach is so lovely it practically looks airbrushed into existence, and somehow this stretch rarely gets too crowded, even in high season. Luxuriate in the trade winds as turquoise water laps at your feet.

12 minutes from central Oranjestad

▶ p66

BEACH BEAUTIES

Conveniently positioned outside the Caribbean's hurricane belt, the ABCs (Aruba, Bonaire and Curaçao) offer mostly sunny skies year-round, making them the perfect destinations for beach bums who relish a great stretch of sand. Aruba's almost-iridescent beaches are the stuff of legend, while Curaçao's have a touch of wildness thanks to dramatic cliffs and coral reefs. Bonaire may not have as many beaches as the other two, but those it does have are charming.

CLOCKWISE FROM TOP LEFT: DIEGOMARIOTTINI/SHUTTERSTOCK, PARKERSPICS/SHUTTERSTOCK, FOKKE BAARSSEN/SHUTTERSTOCK

0 50 km
0 25 miles

Grote Knip

Clear water and dramatic cliffs

One of Curaçao's most beautiful beaches, Grote Knip is a pie-shaped slice of perfection, and it has enough amenities to make it good for families. It does get busy – if you want quiet, head to nearby Kleine Knip.

1 hour from central Willemstad

▶ p198

Caribbean Sea

No Name Beach

A protected eco-beach

No Name sits on Klein Bonaire, the tiny island off the coast of Kralendijk and a protected Ramsar site. Backed by greenery and hemmed in by a stunning coral reef, No Name is a great choice for nature lovers.

35 minutes from central Kralendijk

▶ p138

Klein Curaçao

Porto Mari

Wide-open beach near Willemstad

Porto Mari has something for everyone. Snorkelers enjoy the reefs along the nearby cliffs, while revelers love the amiable bar at the beach's south end. And if you're just here to lounge around, there's plenty of space for that too.

30 minutes from central Willemstad

▶ p199

Te Amo Beach

Bonaire's best sunset

Grab a cooler and watch the sun sink below the Caribbean Sea at the island's best sunset spot. The vibe is jovial – Afrobeats music pumps from small speakers, kids play in the surf and a pleasant chatter fills the air.

5 minutes from central Kralendijk

▶ p140

Bonaire National Marine Park has been under protection since 1979, with strict fishing regulations.

Aruba is home to 10 diveable shipwrecks located along its western coast.

Curaçao's reefs feature 65 different species of coral.

CARIBBEAN ENCOUNTERS

The ABCs harbor some of the best diving in the world. Underwater exploits are frequent and rewarding, no matter what island you're on. Aruba's crystal-clear waters contain fascinating ship dives, Curaçao's calm currents welcome beginners and Bonaire National Marine Park is considered one of the healthiest reefs on the planet.

Left Bonaire National Marine Park (p158) **Right** Snorkeling, Malmok Beach (p78), Aruba **Below** Diving, Bonaire (p158)

→ ARUBA

Most of Aruba's dive sites are only accessible by boat, but snorkelers will still find good underwater opportunities at places like Malmok Beach and Mangel Halto.

▶ Find out more about Malmok Beach (p78) and Mangel Halto (p117)

MICHAEL DEFREITAS CARIBBEAN/ALAMY

CURAÇAO

Curaçao, the Goldilocks of the ABCs, offers a mix of shore and boat dives. One of the most fascinating experiences? A night dive at Rif Sint Marie.

▶ Learn more about Rif Sint Marie (p201)

FROM LEFT: LEX VAN DOORN/ALAMY, TIMSIMAGES.UK/SHUTTERSTOCK

↑ BONAIRE

Bonaire has a whopping 87 public dive sites marked along its ring road, the vast majority of which are accessible from shore for both divers and snorkelers.

Best Sea Experiences

- ▶ **Dive the third-largest shipwreck in the Caribbean, Aruba's SS *Antilla*.** (p86)
- ▶ **Cruise among friendly schools of fish at Curaçao's Director's Bay.** (p183)
- ▶ **Snorkel over shallow reefs at Bonaire's Andrea I and II dive sites.** (p164)
- ▶ **Dive over the steep drop off at Ramsar-protected Klein Bonaire.** (p138)
- ▶ **Snorkel along the coral-covered cliff bases at Curaçao's Kleine Knip beach.** (p198)

National Archaeological Museum

Pre-European history

Aruba had a long human history before Europeans ever set foot here, and this museum investigates how the Arawak and their predecessors lived. The magnificent artifacts on display include ceramic bowls and sculptures crafted during the course of Aruba's human settlement over the past 3500 years.

10 minutes from the cruise-ship terminal

▶ p45

Noord
ORANJESTAD
Aruba
Santa Cruz
Savaneta
San Nicolas

Fort Zoutman

Aruba's colonial era

One of Aruba's signature structures, Oranjestad's Fort Zoutman houses the Historical Museum, whose exhibits illustrate the island's evolution through the centuries. Outside, visitors can see artillery and cannon balls that were once aimed at the bay.

15 minutes from the cruise-ship terminal

▶ p45

Caribbean Sea

HISTORY IN HIGH DEFINITION

These three tiny islands at the bottom of the Caribbean Sea are home to a whole lot of history. Spanish and then Dutch colonial rule left an often painful mark on these places, but today many of the historic sites double as cultural centers, and much is being done to celebrate the unique identity of the ABCs.

Downtown Willemstad

UNESCO-certified streets

The Curaçao capital's downtown looks much like it did centuries ago. Its central neighborhoods (Punda, Otrobanda, Scharloo) have earned a UNESCO World Heritage designation due to the preservation of the buildings along the harbor, which reflect Dutch architecture influenced by the Spanish and Portuguese.

2 minutes from Queen Emma Bridge

▶ p176

Rincon

Bonaire's cultural heart

Kralendijk may house Bonaire's administrative history, but Rincon is where its soul lives. This tiny hamlet is the longest continuously inhabited town on the island, and it's home base for the incredible *krioyo* music scene and Mangazina di Rei cultural center.

30 minutes from downtown Kralendijk

▶ p156

Westpunt
Barber
Kunuku Abao
Curaçao
St Michiel
WILLEMSTAD
Washington Slagbaai National Park
Rincon
Bonaire
KRALENDIJK
Lac Bay
Klein Curaçao

Museum Kura Hulanda

Understanding a difficult past

Curaçao's history is inextricably tied to the terrible legacy of the Dutch West India Company and slavery; the Museum Kura Hulanda delves into the role the institution played on the island, a major transfer port for enslaved people in the Caribbean.

5 minutes from the Queen Emma Bridge

▶ p176

Downtown Kralendijk

Bonaire's colonial history

A walk along Kralendijk's seafront offers insight into the island's varied history – Fort Oranje, the island's oldest stone building, sits on the historic harbor, a stone's throw away from the Terramar Museum, which highlights the island's colonial past and contemporary culture.

2 minutes from the cruise pier

▶ p136

0 — 50 km
0 — 25 miles

Aruba consists of a lava formation and a marine terrace formed by fossilized corals.

Bonaire has dry tropical forest, north; salt flats, south; mangroves, east.

Curaçao features 'diabaas' soil, where smaller plants and rare deciduous trees grow.

HIT THE **TRAILS**

Aruba, Bonaire and Curaçao are covered in vast swaths of what's known as dry tropical forest, a fascinating ecosystem of shrubs, cactuses and evergreens that protect the islands from climate change and erosion – what looks like arid desert at first is actually a vibrant landscape teeming with details that create some really engaging hiking experiences.

Left Natural Bridge (p95), Aruba
Right Arikok National Park (p100)
Below Kibrahacha tree (p16)

→ GETTING THERE

If you're hiking in Aruba's Arikok National Park or Bonaire's Washington-Slagbaai National Park, take a car with decent height clearance – bumpy roads and drainage ditches abound.

▶ Find out more about Arikok National Park (p100) and Washington-Slagbaai National Park (p154)

MULEVICH/SHUTTERSTOCK

GO TREE-SPOTTING

Look out for *divi-divi* (fofoti) trees, bent by the winds, and *wayaká* trees, known as 'trees of life' for the strength of their wood.

▶ Learn more about *divi-divi* trees (p65)

FROM LEFT: YINGNA CAI/SHUTTERSTOCK, GAIL JOHNSON/SHUTTERSTOCK

↑ FIND THE FLOWERS

The ABCs may be arid, but that doesn't mean they don't bloom. *Kibrahacha* trees explode with golden flowers in the summer.

▶ Learn more about *Kibrahacha* trees (p16)

Best Hiking Experiences

- ▶ **Hike the shrubby hills of Aruba's Arikok National Park.** (p100)
- ▶ **Climb to the top of Hooiberg, Aruba's tallest mountain.** (p99)
- ▶ **Encounter five different ecosystems in Curaçao's newest national park, Seru Largu.** (p201)
- ▶ **Walk the limestone cliffs of Curaçao's Shete Boka National Park to see dramatic blow holes and waves.** (p196)
- ▶ **Explore Bonaire's dry forest and learn its history at Washington-Slagbaai National Park.** (p154)

TRADE WINDS

Aruba has constant trade winds year round.

The winds can go up to almost 30mph (50km/h).

The wind has lasting effects on island flora – see the bent *divi-divi* trees.

BOAT **LIFE**

Want to hit the water in the ABCs but prefer to stay above the surface? No need to snorkel or dive for a good time – grab a paddle and explore the islands' bays and coves, relax on a sun-drenched sailboat or cruise to nearby uninhabited islands.

Best Boat Experiences

- **Sail off Aruba's coast in schooners, catamarans and other cruisers.** (p70)
- **Windsurf at Aruba's Fisherman's Hut Beach.** (p80)
- **Kayak among the mangroves at Bonaire's Lac Bay.** (p142)
- **Paddleboard and birdwatch in Curaçao's Spaanse Water.** (p185)
- **Catch a ride out to Klein Curaçao for the day.** (p184)

PHOTOSHOPAV/SHUTTERSTOCK

ABC ARTSY

The Caribbean loves a splash of color, and Aruba and Curaçao take things to another level with dozens of large-scale murals, lively community-centric art festivals and a wealth of independent galleries and museums. Take a tour to learn the stories behind the massive art pieces or beat the heat in breezy art salons.

FROM TOP: GEORG BERG/ALAMY MURAL ART BY JHOMAR LOAIZA, FLAVIO VALLENARI/GETTY IMAGES MURAL ART BY CHEMIS

↑ KAYA KAYA FESTIVAL

Curaçao's **Kaya Kaya Festival** holds events throughout the year, including an art week in May, an ongoing craft market and a street festival in August.

▶ Find out more about the Kaya Kaya Festival (p188)

Best Artsy Experiences

▶ **Walk Aruba's San Nicolas neighborhood and discover murals and sculptures.** (p114)

▶ **Spot sculptures in downtown Oranjestad.** (p44)

▶ **Tour Curaçao's Otrobanda neighborhood for cutting-edge pieces.** (p188)

▶ **Admire art and navigate the Cathedral of Thorns at Curaçao's Landhuis Bloemhof.** (p179)

★ ARUBA ART FAIR

This September event takes over the former industrial town of San Nicolas with gallery showings, fashion shows and new murals.

▶ Discover more about Aruba Art Fair (p114)

This page: Top Mural from the Kaya Kaya Festival (p189), Otrobanda
Bottom Street art, San Nicolas Aruba (p114)
Opposite page Catamaran near Oranjestad (p40)

Summer in the ABCs isn't exactly a low season, but traffic does ease off as temperatures rise and winds slow down.

↘ Turtle-Nesting Season

Summer is the height of turtle-nesting season across the ABCs. Aruba's Dos Playa, Curaçao's Shete Boka National Park and Klein Bonaire are turtle hotspots.

▶ Aruba's Dos Playa p102, Curaçao's Shete Boka National Park p196 and Klein Bonaire p138

← Hills of Golden Yellow

Kibrahacha trees burst into yellow blooms after the first rain following a drought, keeping their flowers all summer.

JUNE

Average daytime max: 32°C (90°F)
Days of rainfall: 1

JULY

Aruba, Bonaire & Curaçao in SUMMER

FROM LEFT: GAIL JOHNSON/SHUTTERSTOCK, ARUBA PARADISE PHOTOS/GETTY IMAGES, STEPHANKOGELMAN/SHUTTERSTOCK, BLUEORANGE STUDIO/SHUTTERSTOCK, TIMARUBA/SHUTTERSTOCK, BOTTOM: SOFINITAA/SHUTTERSTOCK

↘ Aruba International Regatta

Aruba hosts its International Regatta at the end of August, when folks from around the world come out in their sailboats, catamarans, yachts and more.

aruba-regatta.org

Oranjestad

▶ p47

↗ Curaçao Festivals

Curaçao hosts the North Sea Jazz Festival – one of the biggest music events in the ABCs – and the main street festival for Kaya Kaya in August.

curacaonorthseajazz.com

kayakaya.org

Willemstad

AUGUST

Average daytime max: 32°C (90°F)
Days of rainfall: 2

Average daytime max: 33°C (91°F)
Days of rainfall: 3

This season is a bit quiet event-wise, making it a good choice for those who are crowd-averse.

Packing Notes

While weather stays pretty consistent, summer does bring warmer temperatures – always carry water, especially while hiking.

Fall is considered the rainy season in the ABCs, and while showers do pass through, they usually do so quickly, and at night.

↗ Aruba Art Fair

The Aruba Art Fair takes over San Nicolas at the beginning of September, featuring art shows, fashion shows and large-scale mural installations.

arubaartfair.com

San Nicolas

▸ p114

↓ Bonaire Sailing Regatta

The Bonaire Sailing Regatta comes to town in early October, converting quiet Kralendijk into party central.

regattabonaire.com

Kralendijk

SEPTEMBER

Average daytime max: 32°C (90°F)
Days of rainfall: 6

OCTOBER

Aruba, Bonaire & Curaçao in AUTUMN

↓ Hit the Water

September and October are great months to go diving and snorkeling, as the trade winds are quieter and water clarity is good.

↗ Look to the Skies

Fall migrations make the ABCs a great place for bird-watchers: look for ospreys, swallows, sandpipers and yellow-billed cuckoos.

▶ p124

Average daytime max: 32°C (90°F)
Days of rainfall: 7

NOVEMBER

Average daytime max: 31°C (88°F)
Days of rainfall: 9

Hurricanes generally slice through north of the islands, so you'll likely avoid major storms that plague the rest of the region at this time of year.

Packing Notes

We'd say bring your umbrella, but we aren't sure you'll need it, even in rainy season.

Demand for accommodation peaks during winter as folks from colder climes head to the tropics to warm up.

↓ Maskarada

Bonaire hosts the Maskarada on New Year's Day, where masked revelers make their way across the island, musicians in tow.

Bonaire

↗ Christmas & New Year

Christmas and New Year's Eve celebrations define December activities, with calendars filling up with holiday fairs, concerts, parties and more.

DECEMBER

JANUARY

Average daytime max: 31°C (88°F)
Days of rainfall: 8

Aruba, Bonaire & Curaçao in WINTER

FROM LEFT: GAIL JOHNSON/SHUTTERSTOCK, ZMOTIONS/SHUTTERSTOCK, STEPHANKOGELMAN/SHUTTERSTOCK, LUCOP/GETTY IMAGES, AGENTURFOTOGRAFIN/SHUTTERSTOCK, BOTTOM: ERIKA CRISTINA MANNO/SHUTTERSTOCK

↓ Carnival Season

January and February make up Aruba's lengthy Carnival season, with events happening all over the island. Curaçao and Bonaire celebrate in February.

↖ Tumba Festival

Curaçao kicks off its Carnival season with the Tumba Festival – artists compete to make their songs the official anthem of the celebrations.

facebook.com/festivalditumba

Curaçao

Average daytime max: 30°C (86°F)
Days of rainfall: 7

FEBRUARY

Average daytime max: 31°C (88°F)
Days of rainfall: 5

It may still rain in December, but January kicks off the region's dry season, with the chance of rain falling dramatically each month.

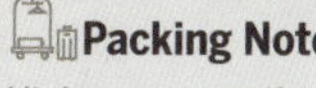

Packing Notes

High season on the islands means one thing, Carnival, so bring your glitter and your party stamina.

Spring marks the end of the Caribbean high season, and while crowds thin out, weather remains consistently warm and sunny, making it a great time to visit.

↓ Krioyo Time

In Bonaire, April is full of festivals and music – Kanto Krioyo takes over stages with its rhythms and everyone heads to the Dia di Rincon party.

Bonaire

▶ p152

↖Color Arrives

Cactuses across the islands begin showing their first blooms – agave, aloe vera, prickly pears and more.

▶ p104

MARCH

Average daytime max: 28°C (82°F)
Days of rainfall: 2

APRIL

Aruba, Bonaire & Curaçao in SPRING

FROM LEFT: LARA RED/SHUTTERSTOCK, DPA PICTURE ALLIANCE/ALAMY, STEPHANKOGELMAN/SHUTTERSTOCK, HORIZONS WWP/ALAMY, SERGEY YATUNIN/ALAMY, STUART WALMSLEY/GETTY IMAGES. BOTTOM: SERGE YATUNIN/SHUTTERSTOCK

→ Curaçao Art Week

The Kaya Kaya Festival holds its Art Week in May, inviting art enthusiasts to peruse local work exhibited in galleries around Otrobanda in Willemstad.

kayakaya.org

Willemstad

▶ p189

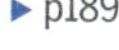

ART BY CHOTA13 HTTPS://WWW.FACEBOOK.COM/SHARE/1CPNVK9BDG/?MIBEXTID=WWXIFR

↓ Catch a Breeze

In Aruba, the Hi-Winds competition kicks off at the end of May, attracting kitesurfers, windsurfers, and kite and wing foilers from around the world.

arubahiwinds.com

Fisherman's Hut

← Curaçao's Seú Festival

Folks celebrate harvest festivals in Willemstad and the Bandabou area in late April and early May.

Willemstad

MAY

Average daytime max: 29°C (84°F)
Days of rainfall: 3

Average daytime max: 30°C (86°F)
Days of rainfall: 2

For all three islands, early March also marks the end of the Carnival season; check local calendars to see when to catch the big finale.

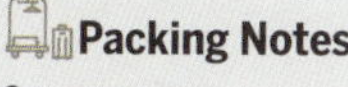

Packing Notes

Sunscreen, sunscreen, sunscreen – spring means nothing but sunny skies and high UV.

DOING YOUR ABCS
Trip Builder

TAKE YOUR PICK OF MUST-SEES AND HIDDEN GEMS

Aruba, Bonaire and Curaçao all sit within one hour's flight of each other, making ping-ponging across islands a breeze. This trip builder wraps the trio's heavy hitters into one spectacular experience.

Trip Notes

Hub towns Oranjestad, Kralendijk, Willemstad

How long Allow nine days

Getting around The only way to get from island to island is via plane, but flights are frequent and relatively cheap. Once you've arrived, you'll probably want a car for the best experience.

Tip Aruba and Curaçao frequently quote prices in guilders, while Bonaire's currency is the US dollar. Pay attention to what currency you're operating in!

Eagle Beach
Admire the fofoti tree and enjoy a magical sunset on the wide sands of iconic Eagle Beach.
10 minutes from Oranjestad

Conchi Natural Pool
Have a wild ocean moment and dive into the clear waters of the rock-lined Conchi Natural Pool on Aruba's East Coast.
30 minutes from Oranjestad

Quadirikiri Cave
Wander the corridors and bask in the skylights of Quadirikiri Cave (pictured bottom right) in Aruba's Arikok National Park.
40 minutes from Oranjestad

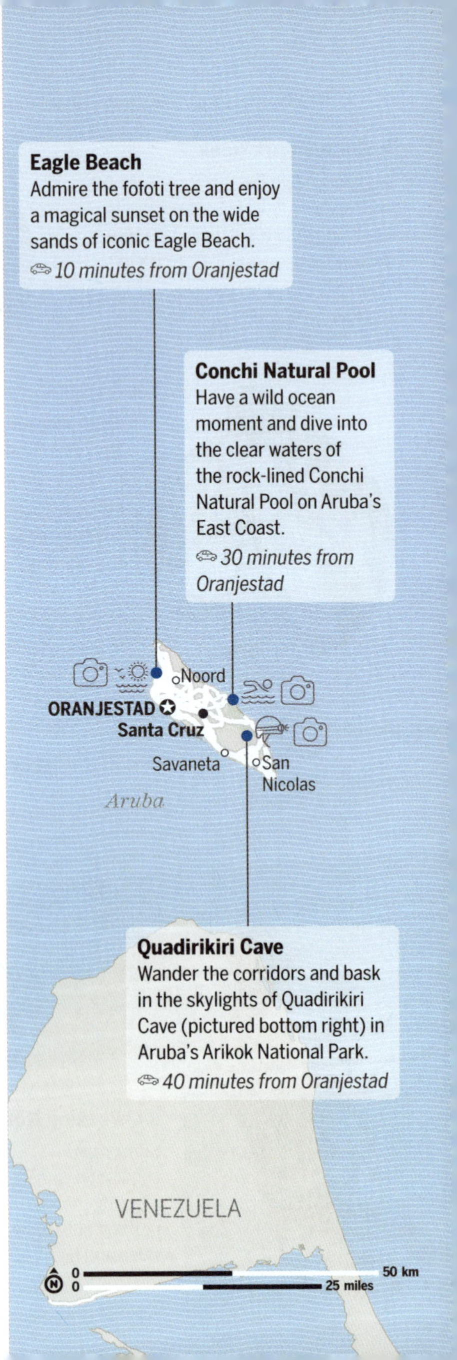

Curaçao's Westpunt
Take a day or two hopping between Westpunt's beaches, like Grote Knip, hemmed in by atmospheric coral-stone cliffs.
50 minutes from downtown Willemstad to Grote Knip

Rincon
Spend some time in Rincon, Bonaire's de facto cultural capital, home to lengthy musical history and the gateway to Washington-Slagbaai National Park.
20 minutes from downtown Kralendijk

Caribbean Sea

Sint Willibrordus
Head to this fertile crescent in central Curaçao to see the island's best terrestrial eco-diversity, learn about its history and lounge on nearby beaches.
30 minutes from downtown Willemstad

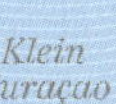

Willemstad
Take a street-art tour through Willemstad's UNESCO-certified core to get a technicolor understanding of today's cultural atmosphere.
25 minutes from Curaçao's airport

Bonaire National Marine Park
Dedicate a couple of days to snorkeling and diving along the stunning reef in Bonaire National Marine Park – see how many different types of coral you can spot! 1000 Steps is a great place to start.
15 minutes from downtown Kralendijk to 1000 Steps

ARUBA
Trip Builder

TAKE YOUR PICK OF MUST-SEES AND HIDDEN GEMS

Sunny, breezy Aruba charms with its beautiful beaches, sparkling resorts and laid-back vibe. Whether you fancy catching a wave in one of the windsurfing capitals of the world, scrambling across arid desert in an ATV or wandering serene national park trails, Aruba's going to win your heart, one way or another.

Trip Notes

Hub towns Oranjestad, Palm Beach, Savaneta

How long Allow a week

Getting around Aruba has a great public-transit system throughout Oranjestad and along the major beach hubs. If you want to go to the northern or eastern sides of the island, however, you'll want a car.

Tip You're generally not allowed to pump your own gas in Aruba; look for the attendant.

Aruba's Shipwrecks
Dive down to inspect the SS *Antilla* (pictured right), one of the many once-seaworthy ships that now lie in the shallows, each with a fascinating story to tell.
Half-day excursion from Resort Area to SS Antilla

Northwest Beaches
Visit the rugged and lesser-known beaches of Aruba's northwest. Spots such as Malmok, Tres Trapi and Fisherman's Hut appeal to active beachgoers who snorkel and windsurf.
18 minutes from downtown Oranjestad to Malmok

Resort Area
Come for the sand, stay for the party – this area buzzes with locals and tourists, and is home to the island's most famous beaches, Eagle Beach and Palm Beach.
15 minutes from downtown Oranjestad

0 — 5 km
0 — 2.5 miles

CLOCKWISE FROM TOP: HUMBERTO RAMIREZ/GETTY IMAGES, YINGNA CAI/SHUTTERSTOCK, ELLENELLERY/SHUTTERSTOCK.

California Dunes
Walk the windswept dunes at Aruba's northernmost point to experience hardcore sci-fi vibes. Alternatively, travel them by ATV.
25 minutes from downtown Oranjestad

Arikok National Park
Explore this rugged national park. It takes up 20% of Aruba's land area, encompassing caves, cactus-covered hills and rugged coastlines.
25 minutes from downtown Oranjestad

Oranjestad
Delve into the pre-European and colonial-era past in central Oranjestad, where there's plenty to keep history buffs interested, including the National Archaeological Museum.
12 minutes from Eagle Beach

Savaneta
Dip your toes in the water lapping at Mangel Halto's mangroves and dig into fresh fish from Zeerover in Savaneta (pictured left), a neighborhood that beckons peace seekers.
21 minutes from downtown Oranjestad

San Nicolas
Admire the murals and hang at legendary haunts at this former refinery town turned open-air art gallery, whose street art has injected major life into Aruba's southern end.
40 minutes from downtown Oranjestad

BONAIRE
Trip Builder

TAKE YOUR PICK OF MUST-SEES AND HIDDEN GEMS

What Bonaire lacks in beaches it makes up for in underwater adventure and big personality. Spend your days floating above one of the healthiest reefs in the Caribbean, learning about Bonaire's history and its lovingly preserved local culture.

Trip Notes

Hub towns Kralendijk

How long Allow a week

Getting around Bonaire's pint-sized landmass is best explored with a car due to lack of public transit and taxis. The main road is in good condition and navigation is easy.

Tip Complete part of your dive training ahead of arrival so you can spend the majority of your time underwater.

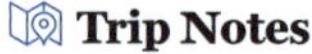

Gotomeer
Spy on powder-pink flamingos as they nest and breed at Gotomeer, the saltwater lake in North End.
35 minutes from downtown Kralendijk

Bonaire National Marine Park
Revel in the wealth of protected underwater marvels at Karpata, a dive site in Bonaire's National Marine Park, which encompasses the entire fringe reef surrounding the island.
25 minutes from downtown Kralendijk to Karpata

0 5 km
0 2.5 miles

Washington-Slagbaai National Park
Wander the cactus-lined trails and boulder-studded beaches of the dynamic Washington-Slagbaai National Park.
35 minutes from downtown Kralendijk

Rincon
Head to Rincon to learn about Bonaire's history and its contemporary culture at Nos Zjilea, a monthly event at Mangazina di Rei.
20 minutes from downtown Kralendijk

Klein Bonaire
Take the water taxi across the harbor to Klein Bonaire, where you can relax on No Name Beach or snorkel the slanted reef.
35 minutes from downtown Kralendijk

Bonaire's Mangroves
Grab a paddle and kayak through the largest mangrove forest in the ABC Islands with the Mangrove Center near Lac Bay.
20 minutes from downtown Kralendijk

Te Amo Beach
Park your beach chair and cooler in the sand and watch the sun go down at friendly Te Amo Beach.
10 minutes from downtown Kralendijk

Sorobon
Learn to windsurf across the smooth, shallow waters near Sorobon, a beach on the southern side of the beautiful Lac Bay.
20 minutes from downtown Kralendijk

Caribbean Sea
Washington Slagbaai National Park
Salina Wayaká
Salina Matijs
Salina Slagbaai
Rincon
Santa Barbara Crowns
Seru Largu
Santa Barbara
Seru Grandi
Hato
KRALENDIJK
Saliña Kangreu
Belnem
Condenser Basins
Pekemeer
Salt Pans

CURAÇAO
Trip Builder

TAKE YOUR PICK OF MUST-SEES AND HIDDEN GEMS

The largest island in the ABC chain, Curaçao ticks all the boxes, balancing adventure with relaxation and offering a thriving capital city for cosmopolitan exploits. Culturally, Curaçao is fostering a new wave of culinary, musical and artistic creativity, making it a fun, forward-thinking place to be.

Trip Notes

Hub town Willemstad

How long Allow a week

Getting around You're definitely going to want your own car to explore all of Curaçao's corners, as public transit outside Willemstad is slow and taxis are limited. Roads are largely in good condition.

Tip Traffic in Willemstad can get pretty dense during morning and evening rush hours; skip driving at peak times to avoid the gridlock.

Cas Abou & Porto Mari
Snag a lounger and spend the day hopping between two of Curaçao's loveliest stretches of sand, Cas Abou and nearby Porto Mari.
45 minutes from central Willemstad

0 — 10 km
0 — 5 miles

CLOCKWISE FROM TOP LEFT: GAIL JOHNSON/SHUTTERSTOCK, GAIL JOHNSON/SHUTTERSTOCK, 49PAULY/GETTY IMAGES

Kleine Knip

Snorkel along the coral-covered cliff bases at Kleine Knip, where you'll spot nimble schools of fish and sea fans waving in the current.

53 minutes from central Willemstad

Shete Boka National Park

Wander along the ocean inlets of Shete Boka National Park to see spectacular blowholes and nesting sea turtles.

50 minutes from central Willemstad

Caracasbaai

Head to Caracasbaai for off-the-beaten-path beach hangs, excellent diving, mangrove paddling experiences and boat rides to neighboring islands.

20 minutes from central Willemstad

Sint Willibrordus

Spot bright-pink flamingos at the saltwater lake near Sint Willibrordus and hike the new national park, Seru Largu.

30 minutes from central Willemstad

Otrobanda

Tour the museums and shops of Otrobanda, Willemstad's street-art hub and the western half of the town's UNESCO-certified core.

15 minutes from central Willemstad

Pietermaai

Make your way to the Pietermaai district in Willemstad for an evening out featuring dinner and drinks at some of the island's most cutting-edge eateries.

11 minutes from central Willemstad

Mambo Beach

In the late evening, make your way down to lively Mambo Beach to dance right on the sand until the wee hours of the morning.

10 minutes from central Willemstad

7 Things to Know About THE ABCS

INSIDER TIPS TO HIT THE GROUND RUNNING

1 Watch Out For The Trade Winds

The trade winds that keep the ABCs more-or-less temperate year-round are a blessing, but also something to consider when planning activities. While they're good for exploits like sailing, landsurfing and windfoiling, they're less ideal for snorkeling and diving. Watch the weather and make sure you're a strong swimmer if you plan to hit the water while the breeze is blowing hard.

2 Take Your Time

Distances across these islands are not long (even on Curaçao, the largest of the three), so you can visit a few different points of interest in any given day. Avoid the temptation to rush, though, especially if you're visiting the national parks – attention to detail is what makes these places magical. Plus, rough roads will slow you down more than you think and cautious driving may save you from a flat tire.

3 The Planes Are Tiny

The planes that fly between these islands are very small, so be prepared for a flying-in-a-tin-can type experience. The airlines are also meticulous about baggage weight, so check restrictions before flying.

4 Dive Smart

Save money by diving during low season – the weather is basically the same as high season and there will be greater availability.

FROM LEFT: BSD STUDIO/SHUTTERSTOCK, RAJADIGITAL/SHUTTERSTOCK, GSAPPHIRE/SHUTTERSTOCK, VERONAWINNER/SHUTTERSTOCK, OLGA 777/SHUTTERSTOCK, KATEPILKO/SHUTTERSTOCK

5 Food Facts

ABC cuisine is an amalgamation of island-grown traditions and Dutch and South American culinary influences: don't miss the *keshi yena* in Aruba (Gouda rind stuffed with spiced meat), the *piská salu* (salt fish) in Bonaire, or the *papaya stobá* (stewed papaya) in Curaçao.

6 Local Lingo

The ABCs are impressively multilingual – on any given day you'll hear English, Dutch, Spanish and Papiamento. The region's creole language, Papiamento (spelled Papiamentu on Bonaire and Curaçao) has roots in Portuguese, Spanish, Dutch and Indigenous and African languages. Dutch and Papiamento are the most common on the ground, with the latter being the most casually used. While you don't necessarily need to know Papiamento to get around, here are some phrases worth knowing:

Bon dia, bon tardi, bon nochi – good morning, good afternoon, good evening

Dushi – the unofficial slogan of the ABCs; it means that something is good, sweet or enjoyable. It can also refer to people, translating as 'my sweet' or 'darling.'

Por fabor, danki – please, thank you

Ayo – a casual goodbye

Bon bini – welcome

Kon ta bai? Mi ta bon – How are you? I'm fine.

Te aworo – see you later

Diskulpame – excuse me

7 Consult The National Parks

The national park entities in Aruba (Aruba Conservation Foundation), Bonaire (STINAPA) and Curaçao (CARMABI) are excellent informational resources before you travel and once you arrive. Consult their respective websites for useful maps and tips, and don't hesitate to talk to rangers on the ground – everyone is happy to help you explore safely.

Read, Listen, Watch & Follow

READ

An Island Away (Daniel Putkowski; 2017) A gritty novel about the refinery days of Aruba's San Nicolas.

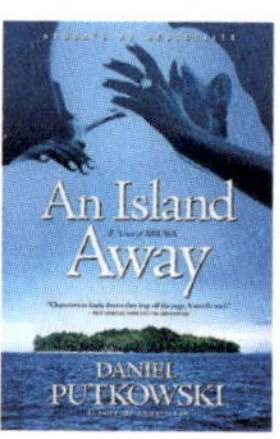

Double Play (Frank Martinus Arion; 1973) Cultural commentary on Curaçaoans and the colonial atmosphere in the 1970s.

Kumbu (Pierre Lauffer; 1996) Poet trailblazer whose work represents the first modernist poetry in Papiamentu.

Nancho van Bonaire (Diana Lebacs; 1976) Children's book about life on Bonaire.

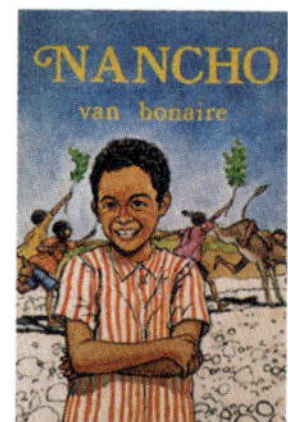

LISTEN

Parranderos (Grupo Di Betico; 1995) Beloved Aruban band specializing in the island's traditional music.

Recuerdonan Stima (Padu del Caribe; 1993) One of the only streamable albums from one of Aruba's most famous artists.

Sero Misericordia (Rich Kalashh; 2021) Most recent album from Curaçaoan hip-hop artist rapping in Papiamentu and English.

Soño di un muhé (Izaline Calister; 2000; pictured) Curaçao icon's debut album, which combines island rhythms with jazz and improvisation.

ROB VERHORST/ALAMY

Tutti Frutti Band Bonaire's folkloric music institution has been serenading the island for 30 years. Listen on YouTube.

WATCH

Abo So (2013) Award-winning musical romance featuring tunes by Aruban singer Padu del Caribe.

Blue Lizard Effect (2024) In-depth travel series on why Aruba is so happy. Terrific visuals and interviews. Find it on YouTube.

Double Play (2017) Adaptation of Frank Martinus Arion's famous novel. Filmed in Curaçao (film premiere at the International Film Festival Rotterdam pictured top right).

Buladó (2020) A magical-realist story examining Curaçao spirituality (pictured bottom right).

Bonaire 48 Hour Film Project (48hourfilm.com/bonaire) Local filmmakers have two days to film stories in Bonaire.

PATRICK VAN KATWIJK/GETTY IMAGES

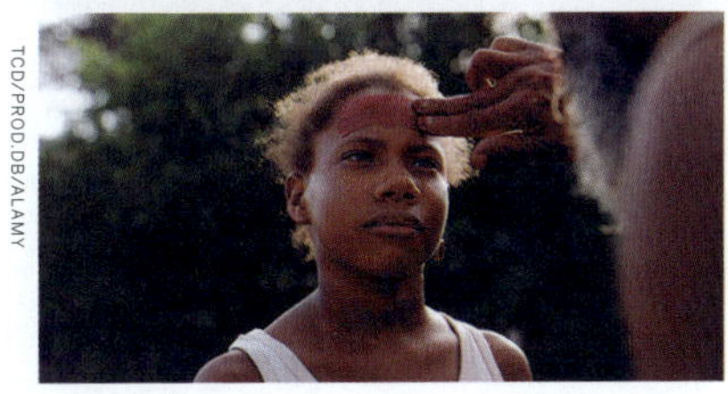

TCD/PROD.DB/ALAMY

FOLLOW

infobonaire.com
Local online publication specializing in news, culture and events across the island.

@arubaeats
Aruba food account with original and crowd-sourced posts about local restaurants.

@chicacaribbean
Curaçao travel tips from a local perspective.

ARUBA

BEACHES | HOTELS | ADVENTURE

RESEARCHED BY ROBERT ISENBERG

NANCY PAUWELS/SHUTTERSTOCK

Practicalities

MAILCAROLINE/SHUTTERSTOCK

ARRIVING

Queen Beatrix International Airport Millions of travelers fly into Aruba's single airport every year. Whether you're arriving from North America, Latin America or Amsterdam, your gateway to Aruba will be this small, navigable complex in the capital city of Oranjestad.

Cruise Ship Terminal Aruba is a favorite cruise-ship destination, and most vessels dock at the Cruise Ship Terminal on the Oranjestad waterfront. Passengers couldn't be more centrally located.

HOW MUCH FOR A

Bottle of Balashi Beer US$2.50

Beach chair rental per day US$10

Bottle of local aloe vera US$30

WHEN TO GO

JAN & FEB
Carnival fever, with music, costumes and parades.

MAR–AUG
Arid summers see the Aruba Summer Music Festival in June.

SEP & OCT
Aruba Art Fair draws artists and collectors from around the world.

NOV & DEC
Winter and holiday tourists pour in.

GETTING AROUND

Car The easiest way to get around Aruba is by motor vehicle, and some places, like Arikok National Park, are nearly impassable without one. Taxis are everywhere in towns and around hotels, and drivers use standardized fares, though few accept credit cards.

Bus Aruba benefits from a comprehensive public-bus system, which connects all major towns. Oranjestad and San Nicolas serve as central hubs; service peters out as you go east. A single trip will cost US$2.60; cash is the most common payment.

ATV Away from towns, road conditions deteriorate. This makes for thrilling off-road adventures on ATVs, UTVs and mountain bikes.

TOP: DARRYL BROOKS/SHUTTERSTOCK
BOTTOM: AL ARGUETA/ALAMY

EATING & DRINKING

Food and drink are the pride of Aruba, and the panoply of options symbolizes the diversity of this busy Caribbean crossroads. Seafood is a local favorite, with fish and oysters served straight from sea. Cafes and bakeries display a rainbow of Dutch pastries, and pan-Latin cuisine is everywhere, thanks to centuries of Spanish influence. For a hearty cholesterol bomb, *keshi yena* (pictured bottom right) is a favorite local dish – a baked mound of cheese stuffed with seasoned meat.

Best nightlife experience Kukoo Kunuku (p71; pictured top right)

Must-try seafood Driftwood (p51)

CONNECT & FIND YOUR WAY

Wi-fi Aruban towns are well connected by wi-fi – much of it free – and consistent cell coverage. SIM cards and roaming plans are easy to secure here, though phone service can get patchy on the East Coast.

Navigation The address system in Aruba is organized and straightforward, with numbers and street names, then the name of the town. Map apps should quickly pinpoint anywhere you need to go.

WHERE TO STAY

Most of Aruba's population lives in the busy northwest, which attracts most of the tourists as well. South Aruba is a quieter option, especially for returning visitors, while the east coast is mostly undeveloped.

Town/Village	Pros/Cons
Oranjestad	Busy, historic and fun to walk, the capital has plenty of shopping and places to stay. Do expect traffic and crowds.
Aruba Resort Area	These opulent estates huddle against immaculate beaches and overflow with entertainment. They can also be generic and pricey.
Savaneta	This town is quieter and more authentic than its northern neighbors; it's also further from a lot of the action.
San Nicolas	South Aruba is full of art and culture, with far fewer tourists than the north. Folks in San Nicolas can be a little earthier as well.

MEDICAL SERVICES

Aruba's main medical center is **Dr Horacio Oduber Hospital**, next to Manchebo Beach. The island is equipped with 10 ambulances and air rescue.

MONEY

One Aruban florin is worth about US$2. Credit cards are accepted at most businesses. ATMs are plentiful around Oranjestad, but hard to find elsewhere.

ORANJESTAD

BUSY | HISTORIC | WALKABLE

RESEARCHED BY ROBERT ISENBERG

Absorb thousands of years of Aruban settlement at the **National Archaeological Museum** (p45)
10 minutes from Cruise Ship Terminal

Explore the ramparts that once defended Oranjestad at **Fort Zoutman** (p45)
20 minutes from Cruise Ship Terminal

Cool your heels on a bench in **Queen Wilhelmina Park** (p53)
20 minutes from Cruise Ship Terminal

Pedal a bicycle along the waterfront on the **Linear Park Trail** (p52). Pick up the trail in Wilhelmina Park, 1km from the Cruise Ship Terminal.
15 minutes from Cruise Ship Terminal

Head to nearby sands and sip a mojito at **Surfside Beach** (p46)
6 minutes from Cruise Ship Terminal

ORANJESTAD
Trip Builder

Oranjestad is the capital of Aruba, and for two centuries, merchants and travelers have dropped anchor in this once-fortified port. The city of 26,000 is also the nation's cultural heart, with its lively waterfront and candy-colored facades.

FROM LEFT: ILDI PAPP/SHUTTERSTOCK, BYVALET/SHUTTERSTOCK
PREVIOUS SPREAD: LITTLE VIGNETTES PHOTO/SHUTTERSTOCK

Practicalities

MONEY

Nearly every store in Oranjestad accepts cards. Common digital payments include Apple Pay and the Dutch Caribbean network Sentoo.

ARRIVING

Queen Beatrix International Airport Most international tourists fly into this airport, 2km from Oranjestad's center.

Cruise Ship Terminal Thousands more arrive here.

CONNECT

Free wi-fi is available in Queen Beatrix International Airport, the Cruise Terminal and many other public spaces.

WHERE TO STAY

Suburb/Area	Pro/Con
Downtown Oranjestad	Close to the waterfront, dining and historical landmarks. Can get noisy at night.
East Oranjestad	Homier hotels in the eastern suburbs, closer to nature. Less walkable and fewer dining options.
Queen Beatrix International Airport	Easy access for early flights. Limited options; scenery less compelling.

GETTING AROUND

Walking Oranjestad is compact and easy to navigate on foot

Taxi It's easy to flag down a taxi. They don't have meters, and fixed fares are based on destination not distance.

Public Bus Oranjestad is the main hub for all public bus routes.

TOP: V. STBAR1964/SHUTTERSTOCK
BOTTOM: APOTEKSPEAKEASY.COM

EATING & DRINKING

Oranjestad is a melting pot of international flavors, from high-end Caribbean fusion to East Asian dishes. Most restaurants are either packed along the waterfront or within a few blocks of the sea. Cruise-ship passengers and overnighters may struggle to choose.

Standout dining experience Yemanja Woodfired Grill (p51)

Best Cocktail Lounge Apotek Speakeasy (p51; pictured bottom left)

ALL YEAR
Oranjestad is active all year, with a tourism spike around the New Year.

JAN & FEB
Aruba's Carnival is a two-month street party, with music and parades.

NOV & DEC
The tourist high season corresponds with North American and European winter.

01 Walk Through HISTORY

ARTIFACTS | SCULPTURES | CANNONS

Oranjestad is the oldest colonial settlement in Aruba, and the city boasts a good number of antique buildings and historical monuments which tell the island's story from the first Spanish arrival in 1499 to the present. In a country mostly known for beaches and resorts, the capital's two major museums offer a rare glimpse into the Caribbean's colorful past.

DBA DUPLESSIS/SHUTTERSTOCK

How to

Getting around: Oranjestad is easily the most walkable place in Aruba, and the museums and fort are all located within easy strolls of each other.

When to go: Both museums are open year-round. The Archaeological Museum is open from 9am to 5pm (closed weekends); the Historical Museum is open 9am to 6pm (closed Sunday and Monday).

Food and drink: Note that neither museum allows food or drink inside.

ILDI PAPP/SHUTTERSTOCK

Far left top National Archaeological Museum **Far left bottom** Queen Wilhelmina Park

Aruba Through the Millennia

Pirate repellent One of the most dramatic structures in Aruba is **Fort Zoutman**, a military outpost erected in 1796 to protect the colonists against invaders. The fort's most iconic appendage is the Willem III Tower, which was built about a century later and did double-duty as a lighthouse and clock; the image of this maroon-and-white tower has come to represent Oranjestad. Housed inside the old walls is the **Aruba Historical Museum**, which uses archival images and period artifacts to illustrate the island's evolution through the centuries. Outside, you can survey the artillery and cannon balls that were once trained on the bay. For the most rewarding experience, visit the fort any Tuesday evening (7pm- 8:30pm; US$5) for the Bon Bini Festival, a lively celebration of crafts, food and performing arts.

Pre-Columbian survey course But what was life like before Europeans arrived? The **National Archaeological Museum** (manaruba.org) displays artifacts excavated from Aruban soil, including ceramic bowls and sculptures, which represent human settlement from the past 3500 years. The man who set local anthropology in motion was a 19th-century priest named Father Antonius Joannes van Koolwijk, who wished to preserve vanishing Indigenous heritage.

The museum is based in a darling green-painted residence which dates back to 1929. Learn how the Arawak and their predecessors survived on this dry island, and crafted objects out of bone, stone and clay.

Sculptures of Oranjestad

Eight sculptures of Blue Horses are scattered around Aruba's capital; they're local artist Osaira Muyale's homage to a legendary herd that broke free from a ship and swam toward shore. Another sculpture, this one depicting a suited man gazing upward, depicts Henny Eman, a local statesman who spearheaded Aruba's secession from Curaçao in 1986. Similar in style and patriotic tone is a sculpture of Padú Lampe and Rufo Wever, composers of Aruba's national anthem, as they huddle around a piano.

Finally, a statue of Dutch Holocaust victim Anne Frank was placed in Queen Wilhelmina Park in 2011, to commemorate the enduring author's birthday.

02 Sun Yourself in THE CITY

CONVENIENCE | FAMILIES | ENTERTAINMENT

Surfside Beach is Oranjestad's own stretch of pearl-white sand. This place is easy to get to, free to visit and full of food and drink options – not surprisingly, it's a favorite among city residents in their off-hours. Start with the usual sunning and swimming, then work your way up to paddling across the crystal-clear waters.

How to

When to go: The beach is open 24 hours. Tan at midday, then grab dinner nearby or go for a night swim with friends. Be aware that lifeguards are rarely posted outside peak hours.

Getting there: From the Cruise Ship Terminal, head southeast along the water for about 1.3km. On foot or by car, you can't miss it.

What to bring: Sunblock, towel, SUP or kayak.

A family favorite Surfside Beach is long and skinny, with a row of cozy hotels and restaurants and a good amount of daytime foot-traffic. Despite its name, Surfside is not known for surfing; the water of Paardenbaai (Paarden Bay) is shallow and the floor is soft, permitting visitors to wade a good distance from the shore. The absence of waves also makes it ideal for young children – you can see the bottom, and the surface will ripple little more than a backyard swimming pool.

Kids can also run free at Neptali Henriquez Park, a playground with traditional plastic structures; note that surfaces can get hot and staticky under a high sun.

You'll usually spot sailboats and catamarans bobbing in the middle distance; come June, the **Aruba International Regatta** (aruba-regatta.org) sets up its Regatta Village right in the middle of Surfside.

HANS WAGEMAKER/SHUTTERSTOCK

Renaissance Island

Across Paardenbaai (Paarden Bay) stretches Renaissance Island, a private ribbon of land owned by the Marriott hotel company. While strong swimmers may be tempted to crawl-stroke out to this attractive barrier island, Renaissance's shores are reserved for guests.

Want to visit anyway? Day passes are available for US$125 per person, and visitors can take a water taxi from the shore to the resort. Wander the beaches, snap close-ups of local flamingos on the Renaissance Island Nature Trail, and grab a bite at Papagayo Bar & Grill. Notable features include hammocks strung over the water and naturally occurring mangroves.

The anytime beach Once you've worked up an appetite, **Barefoot Restaurant** (barefootaruba.com) is right on the sand and serves steaks and seafood from a conical thatched hut.

Next door is **Reflexions Beach Club** (reflexions beach.com), where you can order a piña colada and elevated pub food, then relax in a pool-deck bed.

For dinner, head down the pier to **Pincho's Bar & Grill** (pinchosaruba.com), which has a dining room that hovers over the water and a kitchen serving Caribbean favorites such as seared tuna and cool margaritas.

Above Surfside Beach

Languages of the ABCs

WHERE SPEAKING FOUR LANGUAGES IS CONSIDERED A GOOD START

For more than 500 years, the ABCs have attracted merchants and fortune-seekers from around the world. Each wave of visitors has left its mark on the islands' spoken communication – and created a whole new language, used only here.

Left Carnival in Kralendijk, Bonaire
Center Dushi (p33) sign, Willemstad, Curaçao
Right Sign in Willemstad, with 'welcome' in Papiamentu

ANNA KRASNOPEEVA/SHUTTERSTOCK

Across the ABCs, Dutch is the 'official' language. Local governments carry out their business in Dutch, and most legal documents are first drafted in it too. You may also hear Dutch spoken on the street and in local shops, as an estimated 4500 Dutch-born individuals live in Aruba and more than 9000 in Curaçao. English is also widely spoken, and most Dutch nationals are bilingual in both.

But it won't be long before someone exclaims, *'Bon bini!'*, which you'll correctly assume is not Dutch. It's Papiamento (or Papiamentu), a Creole language that links people across the islands – and is a second official language in both Aruba and Curaçao. (Bonaire officially recognizes it as well.) Papiamento is unique to the Dutch Caribbean, where about 400,000 people speak it fluently.

The Story of Papiamento

Historians believe that the language arrived with Portuguese merchants and the enslaved people they brought from West Africa. The early creole language enabled the Portuguese and Africans to communicate with each other; when the Dutch took over the ABCs in the 1630s, the language evolved further, incorporating words and grammar from Spanish, Dutch and even Arawak. Papiamento was first transliterated in the 1700s and gradually started to appear in hymnals and newspapers.

Unlike many other creole languages, Papiamento is spoken across ethnicities and classes. About 80% of Arubans and Curaçaoans speak it at home, including middle-income households without a trace of African or Portuguese ancestry. By this measure, Dutch is

NANCY PAUWELS/SHUTTERSTOCK

M TIMOTHY O'KEEFE/ALAMY

comparatively rare; only about 13% of Arubans speak it as their primary language, and even fewer Curaçaoans. Papiamento is the preferred idiom for public life and everyday tasks, and once you start keeping an ear out, you'll hear it everywhere.

Polyglot Islands

It's perfectly normal for people in the ABCs to speak at least four languages, reflecting the region's remarkable ethnic diversity. Given the islands' proximity to Venezuela, it's little surprise that the second-most-spoken language is Spanish. English is third, owing to the number of tourists who rely on it during their visits. The ABCs attract an astonishing mix of other languages as well, as travelers arrive from all over the world.

> Papiamento (or Papiamentu) is the preferred idiom for public life and everyday tasks, and once you start keeping an ear out, you'll hear it everywhere.

Some languages have come and gone, of course, or been absorbed fully into Papiamento. Almost no Arubans speak Portuguese on a regular basis, despite its popularity among mariners during the Age of Sail. The original Arawak language, popularly known as Lokono Dian, is essentially extinct here as well; to hear people speak any pure dialect of Lokono Dian, you'll have to visit certain parts of Venezuela or French Guiana, where a minority of Arawak descendants still use it for everyday interactions.

What Should You Speak?

The vast majority of ABC residents speak fluent English, so most North Americans and Western Europeans shouldn't have any problem communicating. Even traffic signs use either English or easy-to-understand symbols and place names.

Papiamento is a point of pride, but no one will expect a tourist to use the language for everyday encounters – offering a phrase or two may delight locals though.

In some places, a little Spanish will go a long way, and if you happen to know a bit of Dutch, some expats may appreciate the chance to use their mother tongue.

03 Knife & Fork FORAYS

CITY VIBE | FINE DINING | NIGHTLIFE

Aruba is full of bars and eateries, but Oranjestad is a place where you can go 'out on the town.' The venerable old streets provide a warm environment for travelers of all stripes, and cruise-ship passengers find diverse dining options the moment they step onto land. Not sure what your taste buds desire? The capital has a little of everything.

NUSA RESTAURANT/NUSA.AW

How to

Getting around: Walking in Oranjestad is easy and fairly safe, even at night. Cabs are also plentiful at most hours.

When to go: Take advantage of those long, near-equatorial evenings. Enjoy sunset dining and late-night drinks in Aruba's big city.

Tipping: The practice of tipping bartenders and service workers varies widely across the Americas, but it's generally expected in Aruba, where 15%-20% of the total tab is a normal sum.

APOTEKSPEAKEASY.COM

Island Bounty

Splurge here Fine dining is an Oranjestad specialty, especially among restaurants within a few blocks of the waterfront. Try **Driftwood** (driftwoodaruba.com), where chef Jovani Rangel's elegant seafood plates are served in a, yes, driftwood-paneled dining room. For ultra fine dining, visit **Wilhelmina** (wilhelmina aruba.com), whose kitchen turns local ingredients into plated artworks, and whose dining room is an Edenic terrace. One of the grandest experiences is **Ever** (ever-restaurantaruba.com), a boutique restaurant right near the water that seats only 14 guests and presents seven-course prix-fixe meals. If you're going to splurge on meals in Aruba, Oranjestad is a natural place to do it, especially if you're staying for a short time.

Taste the world The capital's ethnic diversity is reflected in its culinary scene: On the waterfront you'll find **Nusa** (nusa.aw), an Indonesian restaurant with an explosively flavorful menu. Further inland is **Gostoso Restaurant** (gostoso-aruba.com), which prepares mostly Portuguese classics along with inventive dishes like the criollo sushi roll and chorizo with avocado dip. **Yemanja Woodfired Grill** (yemanja-aruba.com) serves a rainbow of classics, from Thai pumpkin soup to Mediterranean lamb dumplings and Brazilian picanha steak covered in chimichuri butter. Each of these places has a generous drinks menu as well, from imported wines to imaginative cocktails.

Far left top Nusa
Far left bottom Apotek Speakeasy

Capital Libations

Where to grab drinks in Oranjestad is all about what kind of night you want to have.

The **5 O'Clock Somewhere Bar** (5oclocksome wherearuba.com) is your classic sports bar by the water, with pool tables, mini-golf and an open-air atmosphere beneath a protective tent.

A couple of blocks away, **Apotek Speakeasy** (apotekaruba.com) feels like an Edwardian movie set, with its vintage decor and clever lighting; masterful cocktails complete the scene.

Then there's **Café Chaos** (facebook.com/chaos aruba), an atmospheric spot right across from Queen Wilhelmina Park with cash pinned to the walls, bottles of craft beer and a rotating lineup of live bands.

04 Pedal the WEST COAST

LAIDBACK | SIGHTS | INDEPENDENCE

Aruba is small and scenic, and seasoned cyclists have plenty of asphalt and backroads to explore. Regardless of your experience, Oranjestad is a great place to start, thanks to ample bike rentals, flat terrain and the Linear Park Trail, which extends about 3km along the waterfront. Once you adjust to the rhythm of the road, you can crisscross the whole country.

MAILCAROLINE/SHUTTERSTOCK

Trip Notes

Getting around: To get started, the Linear Park Trail is a multi-use path that's bicycle friendly and outlines most of the Oranjestad waterfront. From the western terminus, you can hop onto the highway's separated bike lane to Divi Beach.

When to go: Sunny days and ocean breezes make this route a pleasure any time of year.

Top tip: Slather on sunblock and don't scrimp on water.

Rent a Bike

The **Green Bike** app (greenbikearuba.com) accesses several stations in Oranjestad, along with electric scooters. More personalized options are **EasyHire Tourist Mobility** (arubamobility.com), which rents single-speeds with baskets for US$25 per day, and **TechShack Aruba** (techshackaruba.com), with its diverse fleet of mountain bikes, hybrids and ebikes.

01 There's a Green Bike sharing station right next to the 3D sign spelling out 'Aruba' at **Plaza Turismo**, which is also your gateway to Surfside Beach. Start the Linear Park Trail here.

02 Pause to check out the small, shaded **Boy Ecury Park**, where the Propeller Monument commemorates Arubans who lost their lives protecting the island during WWII.

03 The centerpiece of Oranjestad, **Queen Wilhelmina Park** has manicured lawns and the shops of Renaissance Marketplace next door. Fort Zoutman is also located right around the corner.

04 Turn off the road at the 'I Heart Aruba' sign and step onto the soft sands of **Druif Beach**. Turquoise waters, gentle waves and birds perched on pilings all await.

05 A breezy 5km from where you started, **Divi Beach** marks the start of the resort area, where you can wade into the Caribbean and relax beneath a thatched *palapa*, or palm-covered shelter.

Tanki Flip
Tanki Leendert
Belgiestraat
Driemasterstraat
Emmastraat
Lloyd G Smith Blvd
EasyHire Tourist Mobility
John G Emanstraat
TechShack Aruba
Fort Zoutman
Lagoenweg
Stadionweg
Linear Park
Queen Beatrix International Airport

DESIGNIUM/SHUTTERSTOCK

EWY MEDIA/SHUTTERSTOCK

DUTCH
Architecture

01 St Francis of Assisi Church
This basilica church from 1829 has a fairytale turret and illustrative stained glass above the altar. Services are in English and Papiamento.

02 Queen Wilhelmina Statue
The statue depicts the former Dutch queen in gown and sash. The monarch abdicated in 1948 after ruling 58 years.

03 Casa Rosada
Meaning 'Pink House,' Casa Rosada is a pillared, multi-use building that the Laclé family built in 1904.

04 Willem III Tower
Probably the most recognized structure in Oranjestad, this clock tower was part of Fort Zoutman and served as a lighthouse.

05 City Hall
Other mayors wish their Stadhuis (City Hall) had lime-green walls and bright white balustrades like this showstopper from 1925.

06 Hotel Colombia
This balconied *pension* from 1919 housed guests for decades

before being abandoned. The renovated version houses government offices.

07 Water Tower Oranjestad

Wait, that weird art-deco cylinder is a water tower? Why, yes! It's been among Oranjestad's most distinctive landmarks since 1939.

08 Cas Veneranda

This site is undergoing restoration, but back in 1936, the residence was the design of master Aruban carpenter Dada Picus.

09 Plaza Daniel Leo

The electric-pink, canary-yellow and baby-blue storefronts look like they were extracted straight out of Copenhagen, then brightened.

10 Oranjestad Cemetery

This graveyard is divided into Catholic and Protestant sections, with a Jewish cemetery down the street. Note the above-ground interments.

Listings

BEST OF THE REST

Fun Eats

Bochincha Container Yard $$

This octagonal dining area is composed of eight different eateries, each set inside a former shipping container. Order from any of these windows and find a table in the communal center.

Surfside Beach Bar $$

Set on the edge of Surfside Beach, this sheltered wooden deck redefines convenience. Grab breakfast in the morning, a wood-fired pizza in the afternoon and mojitos in the evening.

Dutch Pancake House $$

Tucked into Oranjestad's oceanside Renaissance Marketplace, the Pancake House turns this traditional breakfast item into a work of art – with over 65 varieties. Tasty for any meal, and pairs well with a rum punch.

Lima Bistro $$$

Stunningly beautiful mains and a marine-inspired interior make this Peruvian restaurant one of the best on the Oranjestad waterfront. Just a three-minute walk from the Cruise Ship Terminal.

Olivia Mediterranean Restaurant $$$

Greek, Italian and Lebanese masterpieces all grace the tables of Olivia, thanks to renowned local chef Dennis van Daatselaar. Don't let the plain facade deceive you; the plant-filled interior is as beautiful as the plating.

Alfie's in Aruba $$

Divey and fun, Alfie's is your go-to spot for craft beer, an oversized burger and a live band or comedy show. Canadian-owned, so you know there's poutine.

Don Jacinto Restaurante & Parrilla $$

This Colombian *parrilla* (grill) has rustic wood tables and festive decor, giving it a down-home feel. You'll find ceviche and empanadas, along with hamburgers and pasta alfredo.

Gateway to India $$

The city's go-to Indian restaurant boasts a family-friendly atmosphere and your classic selection of curries and tandoori favorites. Located just a couple of blocks from the Cruise Ship Terminal.

Kowloon Restaurant Aruba $$

A versatile Chinese restaurant serving a mix of Szechuan and Hunan cuisine, along with Westernized favorites. First opened in 1975, Kowloon is a staple of downtown Oranjestad.

El Chalán $$

The name means 'horse dealer,' referring to Aruba's history as a horse market. Come here for quality Peruvian dishes and seafood in a casual environment.

ALEX CIMBAL/SHUTTERSTOCK

Atlantis VI submarine

Coffees & Snacks

Santos Coffee with Soul $$

The modernist shack near Surfside Beach is convenient for a quick java, but you may decide to linger awhile, thanks to its Spanish tiles, air-conditioning and wide-windowed views of the street.

Aruba Experience Café $$

Like a live-action set for *Encanto*, Aruba Experience has a lovely stone-walled interior, plus original artworks all over the walls. The coffee is excellent and the smoothies to die for.

Island Grind Bochincha $$

Infuse yourself with caffeine from this mural-covered kiosk. Island Grind has three locations, but the adorable little branch on Rockefellerstraat serves joe on the go. Pick up a bag of gourmet beans while you're at it.

Les Cappuchinas $$

On the north side of Oranjestad, Les Cappuchinas is a quirky little coffee shop with grassy walls, a pink sofa and breakfasts so enchanting they could have been prepared by elves.

Smit & Dorlas Coffee House Aruba $$

The brick terrace is a wonderful place to relax on a hot day, especially with a towering frappé in your hand. Many of Smit & Dorlas' coffee drinks are like caffeinated desserts, but leave room for orange rum cake.

Activities

Atlantis Submarines

Ride an honest-to-goodness submarine down to 40m below the surface of the ocean. Large portholes allow you to observe fish flittering past the glass. Atlantis has taken 17 million passengers to date.

J DUQUETTE/SHUTTERSTOCK

Aruba Aloe Factory Museum

George's Cycle Company

Yes, hiking and cycling are fun and all, but an engine will take you a lot further. Tear up the backroads in a UTV with full suspension, or careen around curves on a motor scooter.

Aruba Floating Massage

Careful: an open-air massage on a wood platform floating on gently rolling Caribbean waters might just spoil you for life. But that's the concept behind Aruba Floating Massage. Enjoy this buoyant wellness experience on your own or in pairs.

Aruba Aloe Factory Museum

You've rubbed it on your skin, treated your cuts and knocked back aloe-infused beverages – but how does this miraculous succulent get harvested and bottled? Find out on the Aloe Factory tour, where you can see Aruba's famed flora up close.

ARUBA RESORT AREA

BEACHES | ENTERTAINMENT | PARADISE

RESEARCHED BY ROBERT ISENBERG

ARUBA RESORT AREA
Trip Builder

Beach, dinner, cocktails, repeat. Tourism dominates Aruba's northwest corner, thanks to dreamy white sands and electric-blue waters. Millions converge here every year to chill out by the sea, while millions more strap on snorkels and scuba tanks.

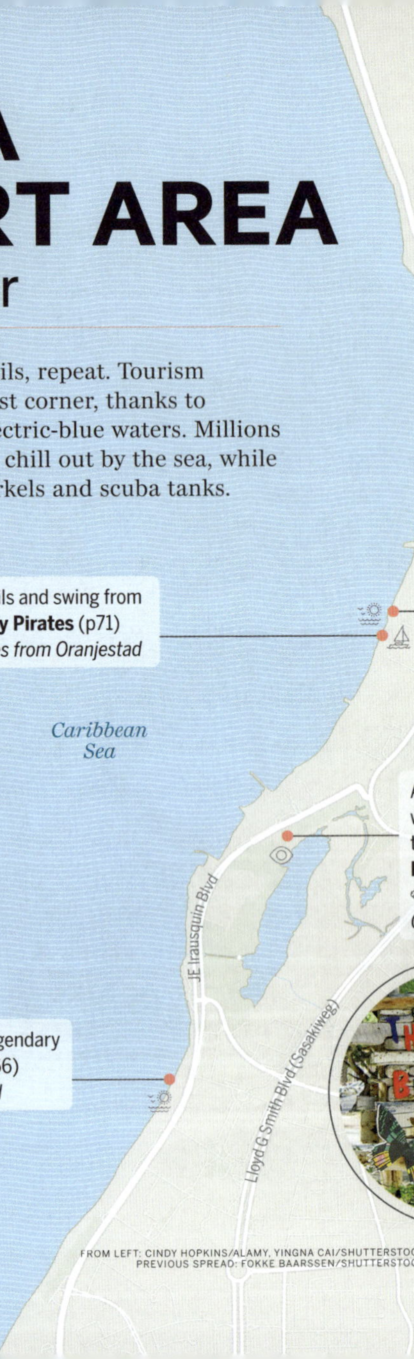

Try your luck at a machine or table game at **Stellaris** casino (p69)
14 minutes from Oranjestad

Sun on the paradisiacal ribbon of sand at **Palm Beach** (p63)
13 minutes from Oranjestad

Clink cocktails and swing from ropes at **Jolly Pirates** (p71)
14 minutes from Oranjestad

Lloyd G Smith Blvd

Caribbean Sea

JE Irausquin Blvd

Lloyd G Smith Blvd (Sasakiweg)

Admire hundreds of winged beauties at the **Aruba Butterfly Farm** (p66)
12 minutes from Oranjestad

Take pictures in front of the legendary fofoti tree on **Eagle Beach** (p66)
10 minutes from Oranjestad

0 — 1 km
0 — 0.5 miles

FROM LEFT: CINDY HOPKINS/ALAMY, YINGNA CAI/SHUTTERSTOCK
PREVIOUS SPREAD: FOKKE BAARSSEN/SHUTTERSTOCK

Practicalities

MONEY

Aruba's resort area thrives on plastic, and just about every hotel and merchant should be able to swipe any major credit card. Cash and digital payments are widely accepted but not preferred.

ARRIVING

While the hotels and resorts in the northwest are, at most, about 13km from the airport, a taxi will cost US$20 to US$30.

CONNECT

Every hotel has free wi-fi, which is usually password-protected and for guests only.

WHERE TO STAY

Beach/Area	Pros/Cons
Palm Beach	The biggest, most action-packed beach in Aruba. Also crowded and pricey.
Eagle Beach	Casinos, resorts and so many restaurants nearby. This quieter locale is a little further from the action.
Divi Beach	Upscale and beautiful, most action revolves around Divi & Tamarijn Aruba Resort

GETTING AROUND

Taxis and shuttles Aruba's northwest is spread-out and suburban. Taxis and shuttles are the norm here, especially among the larger resorts. Organized tours arrange all transport by default.

Car A host of rental-car companies operate out of Queen Beatrix International Airport. Nearly all hotels and beaches have free lots, although parking gets competitive in high season.

TOP: THEOUTERSIGHT/SHUTTERSTOCK BOTTOM: 5PH/SHUTTERSTOCK

EATING & DRINKING

The island's northwest is pure vacationland, and local restaurateurs know what tourists want: flavorful, sit-down experiences with immaculate dining rooms and flowing libations. Seafood, Latin and North American favorites dominate local menus. The Aruba Ariba (pictured bottom left) is the island's riff on rum punch.

Aruba's single craft brewery Fireson Brewing Company (p72)

Must-try seafood Catch Aruba (p72)

ALL YEAR
The resort area runs full-steam all year, but some months are more popular.

APR–AUG
Popularity dips in the driest months, and hotel deals are common.

DEC & JAN
Resorts are most active, drawing crowds from around the world.

05 Wrecks & REEFS

SNORKELING | SWIMMING | SCUBA

Aruba is blessed with some of the clearest waters in the Caribbean, and divers come here from around the world to explore the island's wreath of reefs. The northwest is packed with dive shops and marine-based tour companies, and the waters are rich in wrecks – many of them deliberately sunk to attract underwater visitors.

BLUE-SEA.CZ/SHUTTERSTOCK

How to

Getting around: Beach-goers are welcome to snorkel anywhere near the shore, and as far as they can safely swim out. Organized snorkel and dive tours typically pick you up from your hotel or arrange a rendezvous point.

When to go: Even these crystal waters get a little murkier after a storm.

Equipment: Divers can rent gear from shops; snorkelers will save money by bringing their own mask and fins.

GUSTAVOQUIROGA/SHUTTERSTOCK

JOSEPH PREZIOSO / AFP/GETTY IMAGES

Far left top Sea turtle
Far left bottom Underwater plane wreck
Left Aruba coral reef

Snorkeling basics Throw on a mask and belly-flop into the water anywhere in Aruba – you're bound to see something. If you're still getting used to masks and flippers, the resort area is a calm place to practice, even if there isn't a wealth of marine life. Ready to take on the sea? Palm Beach is full of boats and skippers who will motor you out to the best reefs around. One standout outfit is **Private Snorkeling Aruba** (privatesnorkeling.com), which offers private adult tours on its 8m deck boat. You'll likely spot starfish, colorful surgeonfish, parrotfish and, if you're lucky, a drifting sea turtle.

Just plane wrecked All along Aruba's western shore nearly a dozen wrecks lie at the bottom of the sea. A few of these were victims of circumstance, while others were dumped there on purpose. Each has served as an essential foundation for reef-building, attracting both biodiverse marine life and divers in search of fresh finds. Nearly all lie at depths of 15m or less, accessible to novices and divers with Open Water certifications. The most unusual site is known simply as **The Planes**; the first is a NAMC YS-II turboprop passenger airplane, while the other is a DC-3 destroyed by a hurricane and broken in half. The planes lie just south of Oranjestad but are fairly deep – about 14m at their shallowest points.

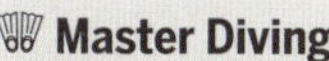

Master Diving

The transparent waters make Aruba one of planet's premiere locations for studying diving. The best-known global authority is the **Professional Association of Diving Instructors** (PADI; padi.com), which is recognized the world over and offers several levels of certification.

To earn your Open Water status, budget three to five days for training and testing. Most dive shops double as schools, and given Aruba's consistently sunny weather and warm waters, the season never really ends.

The majority of instructors will require you to sign up ahead of your visit; also plan a buffer of 24 hours between your last dive and your next flight, to ease pressure changes.

Scan this QR code for more information on diving certification.

06 Embrace the BEACHES

SUN | RELAXATION | WATER

'What's your favorite beach?' This is a question you may hear a lot, as each stretch of sand has a distinct personality. The beaches of northwest Aruba are so sublime, you may want to spend your whole vacation padding down these sun-drenched slivers.

STEVE PHOTOGRAPHY/SHUTTERSTOCK

How to

Getting here and around: The bigger hotels and resorts are located within steps of a given beach. If you want to sample others, a taxi or shuttle is easiest.

When to go: The beaches are busiest in December and January, but any month is near-equatorial perfection.

Seating and cover: Each beach has its own arsenal of umbrellas and reclining chairs, and some offer hammocks and *palapas* (palm-covered shelters) as well.

J DUQUETTE/SHUTTERSTOCK

Three Glistening Kilometers

Palm Beach is the reigning champion of Aruba's resort beaches, thanks to its ivory-white sands – which could take a full hour to cross on foot – plus the row of breeze-bent palm trees that are the beach's namesake. Step into bath-like waters and let your cares evaporate into the bright Caribbean afternoon.

Just beyond the trees, you'll find a veritable wall of high-rise developments, with signs advertising the big-name resorts and casinos. Thousands of guests pour out of these hotels every day to bask in the coastal beauty, which makes for a nice mix of international travelers, yet Palm Beach is also completely public, drawing lots of locals and passersby as well.

The Fofoti Tree

One of the most iconic images of Aruba is the **Fofoti Tree of Eagle Beach**, whose twisted trunk emerges from the sand and branches into a thick plume of leaves. Photograph at will, but don't climb.

FOKKE BAARSSEN/SHUTTERSTOCK

Far left top Druif Beach (p67)
Far left bottom Palm Beach
Above Fofoti tree, Eagle Beach

Selfie Spot

Eagle Beach is one of the most renowned in the world, thanks to its perfect white sand, warm cyan-tinted waters and palm trees. At 1100m across, it looks almost like a movie set for a tropical paradise, yet somehow this stretch rarely gets too crowded, even in the high season. One virtue is its primo location, just south of the biggest resorts and just north of Oranjestad's sprawl; nearly all the development lies across JE Irausquin Blvd, making the many hotels and restaurants feel further away than they are.

Southern Escapes

Divi Beach occupies a ritzy little bulge of land to the south of Eagle Beach, sharing the latter's blissful aesthetic but attracting fewer visitors. This area is best known for its high-end property, the **Divi Aruba All Inclusive Resort** (diviandtamarijnaruba.com), which doubles as a luxury hotel and an 18-hole golf course,

Frolic with Butterflies

Lepidopterists, rejoice! Just south of Palm Beach stands the **Aruba Butterfly Farm** (thebutterflyfarm.com), an indoor preserve containing hundreds of hueful specimens. Established in 1999 by owner William Slayter and several collaborators, the farm draws butterflies from across the Americas. Guided tours last about 25 minutes, but you're welcome to cavort with these ethereal insects for as long as you like, fortified by a bite from the on-site snackbar.

Curiously, the Butterfly Farm in Aruba is a sequel venture to the original, based on the island of St Martin, which was tragically destroyed by 2017's Hurricane Irma.

Scan this QR code for more information about the butterfly farm.

The Links at Divi Aruba, which is the nation's largest. The resort is a dream, with both pool-view and ocean-view rooms, plus easy access to the waterfront. That said, Divi Beach is public, so non-guests can roam this subtle surf as well. Divi's twin is **Manchebo Beach**, a sublime half-moon flanked by resorts and punctuated by cactus, just south of Eagle Beach. The two beaches flow into each other, but the division is marked by the chill **Coco Loco Beach Bar** *(facebook.com/cocolocobeachbar)*.

Closer to town is **Druif Beach**, a 300m-long bow of sand. The beach starts less than 3km from the Cruise Terminal, so visitors to Oranjestad can easily walk or bike there. Both Divi and Druif are great spots to spread out a towel and watch pelicans dive for fish, or string up a net and play pickup volleyball. At the northern end of Druif stands **Bunker Bar**, an octagonal hut that's built over a former WWII fortification and is part of the Divi & Tamarijn Resort.

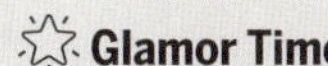

Glamor Time

If you're seeking some action, Eagle Beach is just a short walk from **Glitz Casino** (p73) and the luxurious **Eagle Aruba Resort**.

FROM LEFT: SUNSHINE ON MY SHOULDERS/SHUTTERSTOCK, ANHILATOR/SHUTTERSTOCK

Left Aruba Butterfly Farm
Above Manchebo Beach

07 Get ACTIVE

WIND | SEA | GAMES

Once you've reclined on the beach, polished off some fruity cocktails and eaten your weight in mahi-mahi, you may be ready for some action. The resort area knows just how to occupy its guests – with watersports, nautical jaunts and a tall stack of poker chips. On the sunny shore or inside an air-conditioned resort, thrills await.

How to

Getting there: Resort area beaches are some of the easiest-to-reach destinations in Aruba: go west until you hit them. Parking around the beaches is busy and expensive; walk, taxi or bike if you can.

When to go: Mornings are coolest, afternoons are hottest, but the water is refreshing anytime. Take the usual precautions after dark.

Towels: No need to bring beach towels; hotels usually provide them, especially if you're staying near the beach.

Feel the Burn

If you thought regular aerobics was hard, you should try it on a trampoline. **Energy Fit** is Aruba's one and only 'jumping fitness studio,' where patrons of all ages and abilities synchronize their movements on small, personalized launchpads. Pop in for a free trial session, and if you plan to stay on the island for awhile, consider a four-class package.

For a quieter experience, head over to **Happy Buddha** (happybuddha-aruba.com), one of the resort area's only brick-and-mortar yoga studios. Join a Hot Hatha class (maximum 20 participants) or sign up for a private yoga or meditation session. After, take a picture in front of the studio's trademark mural: a smiling Buddha holding a rainbow.

What Floats Your Boat

There is no shortage of boats around here, but

what sets **Octopus Aruba** (octopusaruba.com) apart is its sheer range of watercraft, from a catamaran to a private speedboat.

Private sailing charters will take you onto the water at any time of day, including during those otherworldly sunsets.

The lovely addition to the Octopus fleet is its Aqua Donut Boat, which looks like a gigantic pool toy with an overhanging umbrella. The advantage of the Aqua Boat is that you can rent it out for two-hour outings – and bring up to nine of your friends – without requiring a captain.

Roll the Dice

Games of chance are legal in Aruba, and the west coast is thick with casinos, most of them clustered along Palm Beach. The largest is **Stellaris** (stellariscasino.com), which is housed in the Aruba Marriott Resort.

This massive complex maintains 400 slot machines and 17 gaming tables, along with kiosks for sports betting and a VIP club for regulars. Drinks are served across the gaming floor, and the complex has several restaurants to choose from. If you're 18 or older, all you need is a valid ID to join in the fun.

Scan this QR code for more information about Stellaris.

Above Octopus Aruba

08 Parties, Bars & FESTIVALS

DRINKS | MUSIC | DANCING

Aruba is one of the Caribbean's nightlife capitals, and the resort district is its beat-blasting, shot-pouring, disco-lit epicenter. Each hotel has its home-grown entertainment, so you don't have to stray far from your room. Other visitors like to hop around the district, sampling bars and clubs from Oranjestad to Arashi Beach. However you like to party, Aruba is one happy island.

JAN-OTTO/GETTY IMAGES

How to

Getting there: For boozy nights on the town, taxis are generally safe and plentiful. Many resorts and hotels are within easy walking distance of local entertainment as well.

When to go: The party never stops in Aruba, but major concert events, like the Aruba Soul Beach Music Festival (May) and Aruba Summer Music Festival (June), draw colossal crowds.

Cover charges: Some of the bigger clubs charge a modest cover charge, so bring cash.

BAMBI2020/SHUTTERSTOCK

SOLARISYS/SHUTTERSTOCK

Far left top Aruba Carnival
Far left bottom Kukoo Kunuku party bus
Left Jolly Pirates Aruba schooner

Captain for a night No one brings a party like Caribbean buccaneers, and **Jolly Pirates Aruba** (jolly-pirates.com) is no exception. The schooners are designed to look like galleons and sail along Aruba's coast, serving 'grub and grog' along the way. Shipmates are treated to an open bar, bottomless barbecue and live DJs; meanwhile, you're welcome to leap in the sea – or swing on a rope into the sea – whenever you feel the urge. While Jolly Pirates specializes in sunset cruises and private parties, the ships are also designed for daytime swimming and snorkeling excursions, which welcome children as well. Among other sustainable touches, the company uses compostable cups.

Charter and chug One look at the watermelon-colored **Kukoo Kunuku** (kukookunuku.com) party bus and you'll know you're in for a wild time. Kukoo Kunuku transports tourists all over the island, and the activities are wide-ranging: there's the Cultural Island Tour to Baby Beach and the Wine on Down the Road tour of local restaurants that specialize in wine. But this outfit is best known for its rambunctious bar-hopping, such as the Pub Krawl, the Kukoo Happy Hour and, at the start of the year, the Carnival Experience. Participants have to purchase most of their beverages when they arrive, but Kukoo offers festive company, a designated driver and curated nightlife. No reason to dress up; these excursions are 'Kukoo casual.'

Carnival

Steel-drum bands. Parade floats. Costumes bursting with colored feathers. **Aruba Carnival** is a nationwide festival that takes up most of January and February, and everyone is invited. Taking inspiration from carnivals across the Western Hemisphere, Aruba's version kicked off in 1954 and has grown exponentially since then, incorporating a wild spectrum of music and vestments.

Carnival technically starts on November 11, but the biggest events are scheduled for after the New Year: the Calypso Roadmarch Contest, the Grand Queen Election, the San Nicolas Children's Parade, and, finally, the Grand Carnival Parade through Oranjestad on March 1.

Listings

BEST OF THE REST

Drinks

Pega Pega $$

This beach-facing grill is the pride of the Manchebo Beach Resort, and the atmosphere only gets better after a trademark sunset and a few expertly mixed cocktails.

Saloon Bar $$

Stained-wood surfaces, a cow's hide stretched across a wall and a slew of craft beers – this place has earned the moniker 'saloon.' The music is always good, even on karaoke nights.

Mambo Jambo $$

Margaritas, coconut martinis and watermelon mojitos in a Latin eatery that puts a colorful spin on tropical drinks. The menu serves up global platters as well, from carpaccio to tuna tataki.

Humidor $$

This cigar bar's collection has stogies from across Latin America, including a robust Cuban selection. Pair with cognacs and bourbons in a decadent little alcove.

Fireson Brewing Company $$

There is only one brewery in Aruba, and Fireson is it. Owners Radinka and Tony van Vuurden named this hip tasting room after their son. IPAs, stouts, saisons, you name it.

Eats

Bugaloe Beach Bar & Grill $$

Start your morning with French toast, devour a noontime burger and enjoy drinks and live music till midnight. Always active, this thatched-roof entertainment hub sticks far out into the water.

Azia Restaurant & Lounge $$$

Feast on Mongolian beef on an outdoor terrace festooned with lights. The high-quality pan-Asian menu attracts lots of regulars, and the long, beautiful bar may keep you out till midnight.

Ceviches Pool Bar & Restaurant $$

Plenty of travelers define 'vacation' as sipping mimosas by the pool – you can do that here. The sandwiches, wraps and, yes, ceviche make this place a solid restaurant.

Catch Aruba $$$

Beautiful cuts of fish grace every dish in this revered seafood restaurant. A welcoming green patio and live entertainment keep the upscale venue inviting and fun.

Craft $$

With gourmet coffee, fun cocktails, fusion breakfasts and healthy açai bowls, Craft lives up to its name, but it's also an affordable spot for all three meals (plus Taco Tuesdays).

Gianni's Ristorante Italiano $$$

A giant statue of a chef looms over a fountain as you enter this veritable emporium of fine Italian. Gianni's is atmospheric, beautifully decorated and absolutely aces grilled branzino.

Dive Shops

Palm Beach Divers Aruba

Formerly known as Diversity, Palm Beach takes small groups of all skill levels, including first-timers, experts and PADI-certified divers looking for a refresher course.

Divers of Poseidon

This budget outfit introduces newbies to diving, rents out equipment to indie divers and even provides specialized training for aspiring underwater medics. Snorkeling and fishing trips also available.

Mermaid Divers Aruba

A pillar of the Aruban diving community that has taken first-timers to reefs and trained certified divers since 1990. Hotel pickup is provided, along with all equipment. Packages include up to 11 dives.

ScubaCaribe

True to its name, this company has built a diver-training empire across the Caribbean and Africa. Multilingual guides, standardized equipment and more than 30 years of experience lend the brand a lot of authority.

Aruba Dive 4 Life

Operated by local dive instructor Marcel Maduro, Aruba Dive 4 Life is a small business that takes divers to any reef on the west coast.

Casinos

Casino at the Ritz-Carlton

This sizable casino off of Palm Beach covers nearly 1400 sq m of machines and gaming rooms, including 14 traditional table games. Redeem points for dining or spa treatments.

Alhambra Casino

As part of the gigantic Divi Aruba All Inclusive Resort, this place has everything: 450 machines, a range of table games, card lessons and a multi-tiered Players Club. Enjoy live entertainment and easy access to Divi Beach.

Glitz Casino

Hop around machines and table games, and enjoy themed events and holiday specials. Glitz is a casual casino tucked into La Cabana Resort on the north side of Palm Beach.

Casino at Hyatt Regency

Covering an impressive 1040 sq m, the Hyatt Regency casino offers 13 gaming tables,

DIEGOMARIOTTINI/SHUTTERSTOCK

Casino at the Ritz-Carlton

192 slot machines and 15 video poker screens. Try your luck between treatments at the resort's spa.

Liv Casino

Right in the middle of the Palm Beach resort district, Liv Casino is the centerpiece of this beloved Barceló hotel property. Hit the machines, practice your poker face and enjoy live entertainment.

Outdoor Adventure

Frank's Place Watersports

We dare you to find a water-based activity that Frank's can't accommodate. Come here for wave-runners, tube rides, water trampolines and banana boats, among other activities and rentals.

Julio's Watersports Eagle Beach

Always wanted to parasail but weren't sure where and when? Julio's Watersports will make all the arrangements. Chickening out? No problem; staff also provide chairs and umbrellas on Eagle Beach.

Delphi Watersports

Just when you had given up on your dream of flying over the water in a jetpack, along comes Delphi. Try other high-tech toys like flyboards, jetovators and waverunners as well.

THE NORTHERN COAST

BEACHES | DUNES | LANDMARKS

RESEARCHED BY ROBERT ISENBERG

NORTHERN COAST

Trip Builder

The northern tip of Aruba is a wide-open landscape of windswept dunes, secluded beaches and a lattice of informal trails. This district is part of Aruba's 'Noord' (Dutch for 'North') and offers visitors quiet residential neighborhoods and scattered luxury pleasures.

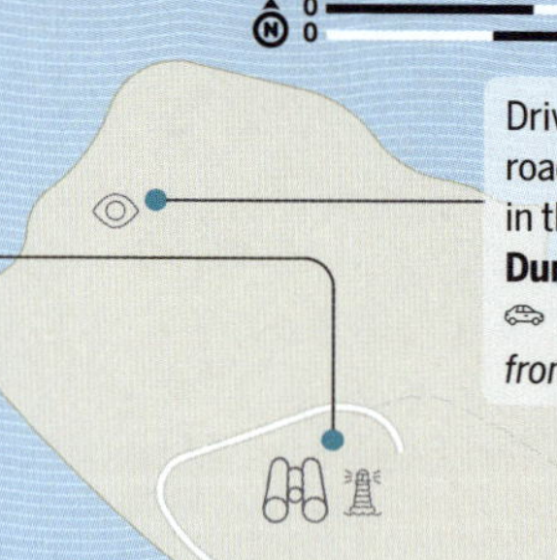

Climb to the top of the historic **California Lighthouse** (p83)
25 minutes from Oranjestad

Drive along dirt roads on an ATV in the **California Dunes** (p82)
20 minutes from Oranjestad

Snorkel amid sea life in the rocky waters of **Tres Trapi** (p78)
20 minutes from Oranjestad

Explore the rusted underwater hull of the **Antilla Wreck** (p86)
30 minutes from Oranjestad

Learn windsurfing basics in ideal conditions at **Fisherman's Hut** (p80)
15 minutes from Oranjestad

FROM LEFT: DASZA/SHUTTERSTOCK, DARYL DUDA/SHUTTERSTOCK
PREVIOUS SPREAD: FOKKE BAARSSEN/SHUTTERSTOCK

Practicalities

MONEY

Cards are universally accepted at hotels and restaurants. Cash is less common, and ATMs are nonexistent.

ARRIVING

From **Queen Beatrix International Airport** you're only 25 minutes from any northern motorway. From Oranjestad the L10 bus goes as far north as Arashi Beach.

FIND YOUR WAY

GPS is handy up here, as even well paved routes can twist into knots.

WHERE TO STAY

City/Area	Pros/Cons
Esmeralda Westpunt	Most hotels are clustered around this inland development. The area feels quiet and remote.
Aruba Resort Area	The vast majority of tourists stay just a few kilometers south. Convenient, but busy.
Oranjestad	The capital isn't far away, and it's a great base camp; also crowded.

GETTING AROUND

Car Developed areas in the north are easiest to access by car, but you'll want a 4WD to tackle the dunes' rough backroads.

ATV Thanks to their thick tires and full suspensions these vehicles are ideal for the California Dunes, either on your own or as part of an organized tour. You'll also fare well with other durable vehicles, like UTVs and mountain bikes.

TOP: JEFFREY R DARBY/SHUTTERSTOCK
BOTTOM: ASHOK SAXENA/ALAMY

EATING & DRINKING

Most visitors to Aruba's north end up returning to Oranjestad or the resort area, as this part of Noord is a food desert. The district does have a handful of eateries with pub and Caribbean fare.

Best Italian Faro Blanco Restaurant (p88; pictured top and bottom left)

Great Dining & Drinks Restaurant at Tierra del Sol (p88)

ALL YEAR
There's never a bad time to visit the north. Weather stays fairly consistent throughout the year.

JAN & FEB
The northwest is a quieter place to stay during Carnival.

OCT–DEC
A little rain adds color to the landscape.

09 Northwest BEACHES

QUIET | RELAXATION | EXPLORATION

Swimming, sunning and snorkeling – you'll find all three in the north of Aruba, but with a fraction of the traffic. These four beaches feel like a well-kept secret, though they're all within strolling distance of the nation's most opulent resorts. If you trust your swimming skills and pack your own lunch, these northern escapes promise tranquil hours in and on the water.

How to

Getting there: From the resort area, all these beaches are quick to reach by car, bicycle or on foot.

When to go: If you're truly seeking out solitude, early mornings and weekdays are best, as most beachgoers will start trickling in later in the day and at weekends.

Don't forget your goggles: Whether you're properly snorkeling or just want to see underwater, these beaches ease into outrageously clear waters.

Not quite 2km past the hubbub of Palm Beach, you'll find the peaceful little niche known as **Malmok Beach**. Slip down the limestone rocks that cradle this spot and wade out into calm waters. Malmok is a 700m stretch of brown-tinted sand and pebbles, and it's a favorite among fishers and casual swimmers.

This area feels remoter than it is, as the beach is undeveloped, and the nearest structures are a housing development across the road. Note that there are neither lifeguards nor amenities, so splash around with caution.

The next beach up is **Tres Trapi**, a rocky little inlet popular with snorkelers. The short cliff drops off abruptly into the water – which is why someone thought to carve steps directly into the rock.

Right next door is **Boca Catalina**, a rustic stretch of

SABRINA ERNST/GETTY IMAGES

grass, coral rock and sand. Both are easy to access, with roadside parking, free entry and only scattered beachgoers to share the scenery with.

A number of shelters are already set up here, making it the perfect spot for a quiet dip or beach read.

The northernmost destination is **Arashi Beach**, a blindingly white crescent that measures only 300m in length. Still, you'll find everything you need for a beach day: parking, chairs, *palapas* (palm-covered shelters) and even the local snack bar.

Vessel Vestige

Just 100m away from Malmok Beach, the rusted hull of the **Baboo Shipwreck** pokes out of the water. The ship was deliberately sunk in an effort to build up reefs and give divers a playground to explore, but Hurricane Lenny pushed the ship closer to land in 1999.

Today, strong swimmers can crawl-stroke to the wreck and snorkel around its decomposing frame. Take care around the Baboo's sharp edges and amid the water's powerful riptides.

True to the original mission, the vessel attracts populous schools of fish, and you don't need a boat or special equipment to visit.

Above Malmok Beach

10 Watersports at HADICURARI

WIND | SEA | SAILS

Aruba boasts some of the best windsurfing conditions in the world. Even if it's a new concept to you, there's no better place to learn than Hadicurari Beach, better known as Fisherman's Hut. Here you can take a lesson, rent equipment and hone your breeze-harnessing skills on picture-perfect waters. You can also sample a range of other watersports, from manual to motorized.

How to

Getting around: Fisherman's Hut is thick with watersports shacks, and you can easily walk from one to the next. The beach is also an easy drive or bus trip from downtown Oranjestad.

When to go: Lessons get harder to book in the high season; you'll have the most flexibility from March to September.

Look both ways: The waters along Fisherman's Hut can get busy with windsurfers, boats and swimmers.

Catch the Breeze

For windsurfers, the **Fisherman's Hut** coastline provides a perfect balance of calm waters and consistent breeze; the water remains only chest-deep for 500m out to sea, so most adults can wipe out and recover without needing to tread water. The conditions are also ideal for kiteboarding, which is wildly popular here too. On any given day, the skyline is bustling with fast-moving triangular sails and kiteboarders getting pulled along the waves by their parachute-like kites.

This little beach is home to several rental companies and training centers, and the fun begins the second you paddle out into the water. Rent windsurf equipment or take a lesson with **Blue Highway Aruba** (windsurfing aruba.com), or head nearby to **Vela Sports Aruba**

EGT-1/SHUTTERSTOCK

(velaaruba.com) for kite-surfing, e-foiling and stand-up paddleboard yoga.

Power Sport

How about trying wind-foiling? Here, a hydrofoil is affixed to the bottom of the board, so you and your sail can hover above the water.

Aruba Active Vacations (aruba-active-vacations.com) will help you fly through the air with its state-of-the-art equipment. It also offers instruction in kiteboarding and other watersports as well as a fleet of 'blokarts', or wind-powered go-karts if you want to stay on dry land.

Beach Yoga

Aruba Kitesurfing School (arubakitesurf.com) is a one-stop shop for outdoor sports. You can rent a stand-up paddleboard, snorkel at sunset or rent an ATV – along with, of course, kitesurfing lessons.

One of its spinoffs is **Beach Yoga Aruba** (beachyoga aruba.com), which provides outdoor wellness sessions right on Hadicurari's sands. Join a class, request private coaching or restore yourself with a sound-healing session.

While Fisherman's Hut is best known for its high-octane sports, Beach Yoga Aruba will re-center you with stretching, meditation and, once a month, a full-moon yoga class. You really won't find a more beautiful spot for sun salutations.

Above Kitesurfing, Hadicurari Beach

11 Explore the DUNES

SAND | OFF-ROADING | LIGHTHOUSE

Hike Sahara-like dunes. Climb to the top of a Victorian lighthouse. Careen around dusty backroads. While others catch a tan, restless travelers will find countless heart-pounding activities to fill the afternoons. Head to the California Dunes for dusty outback adventures.

How to

Getting there: Whether you book a tour or go solo, getting around northern Aruba is half the fun. Drive a rental car, hire an ATV or explore on foot.

When to go: From October to January there's always a chance of rain, which may put a damper on outdoor activities.

Bring supplies: There's almost no development beyond Arashi Beach, so carry in water and food.

All-Terrain Outings

The northern edge of Aruba looks like a classic desert, and it's hard to tell exactly where the eastern **California Dunes** end and the central Sasariwichi Dunes begin. Unpaved roads wind their way through this primal terrain, which is ideal for ATVs and their even brawnier cousins, UTVs. Close to the dunes is **Arubiana** (arubiana.com), which rents out both types of vehicles as well as Vespa scooters. Riders 18 and older can rent for four- or eight-hour sessions and drive just about anywhere on the island; a driver's license from your home country is required.

Take a Hike

A less technical option is simply to hike the **Westpunt Trail**, roughly a 4km walk through the northern reaches. The trailhead lies just north of Arashi Beach,

IGAL SHKOLNIK/SHUTTERSTOCK

and you can follow the footpath along the sea-spraying northern coast. Improvise along trails and dirt roads that meander through the silty white dunes and patches of scrubland.

A common endpoint is **Westpunt Beach**, an undeveloped segment of sandy flats and smooth boulders. Free to visit, Westpunt has a flair for the dramatic, with its whipping winds and crashing waves.

A bonus to the California-Sasariwichi Dunes is that it's almost impossible to get lost; just head south through the barrens and it's only a matter of time before you hit a paved road.

Aruba's Beacon

You'll see the **California Lighthouse** from kilometers away, a slender white spire rising 30m above the arid landscape. Take the paved road right up to its base, where there's always plenty of parking. Originally built in 1910, the lighthouse is now open to visitors between 9am and 7pm, and for US$5 you can climb its spiral staircase to the top, peering through staggered windows as you ascend. The 360-degree views from the upper platform are outstanding, and extra netting over the guardrail should reassure visitors afraid of heights.

The best time to visit? During one of the Caribbean's sky-blazing sunsets.

Above Westpunt Beach

12 Big Skies of the NORTHEAST

OUTDOORS | SOLITUDE | GOLF

The northeast coast is one of the least-visited crannies in all of Aruba, and you may feel a little like Robinson Crusoe when venturing into this lightly settled land. This is a place for spending hours outside. Much of the interior is taken up by the undulating turf of a golf course, while the copper-colored fringes show only the subtlest hints of human visitors.

STEVE MURRAY/ALAMY

How to

Getting around: None of these destinations are far from the resort area, and you could theoretically reach them on foot or mountain bike. Most people, though, will take these quiet roads in a rental car or on the back of an ATV.

When to go: Mornings are coolest, which can be a godsend in a landscape with so little shelter.

Wear sunscreen: The intensity of the Aruban sun can't be overstated.

AMY CICCONI/ALAMY

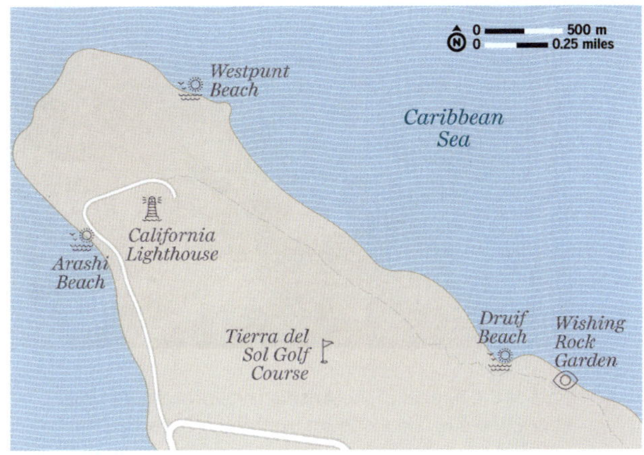

Far left top Tierra del Sol Golf Course
Far left bottom Wishing Rock Garden

Fore! The lush green fairways of the **Tierra del Sol Golf Course** look completely out of place in the burnished terrain of northwest Aruba, yet by some miracle – and clever irrigation – this recreational oasis has hosted foursomes since 1995. It's is the only 18-hole golf course in the country, and it has long been busy with world-class tournaments.

As luxurious and exclusive as this gated community may seem, the Tierra del Sol country club charges shockingly low membership fees, and any passing traveler is welcome to reserve a tee time on its website (starting at US$99). The grounds started undergoing a complete renovation in 2024; as of this writing, only a nine-hole course is available while improvements are still being made but they were due to fully reopen by the end of 2025.

The other Druif Wait, are you seeing double? Isn't **Druif Beach** on the west coast, not the east? As it happens, Aruba has a second sandy spot, not quite 2km down the road from the California Lighthouse. 'Druif' is Dutch for grape, which doesn't really explain either name, but no matter; this beach is also modest, quiet and far less visited than other east coast locations.

The coastal drive is spectacular, with waves crashing against the rocky shore and rolling bluffs all around. Unlike the western Druif Beach, this is a prime spot to try some surfing.

Wish upon a Stone

As you drive south from Druif Beach, you will spot a cluster of cairns. Not just a few cairns or even a dozen, but hundreds of stacked rocks spread out across the parchment-colored soil.

This mysterious place is the **Wishing Rock Garden**, where each little stone pile represents a wish. No one knows exactly where this distinctly Aruban tradition comes from, but the garden follows the same logic as a wishing well: if you make a little sculpture out of stones, your most heartfelt desire will come true. The garden is free to visit, but do make sure not to topple anyone else's wish.

The Antilla Wreck

WHERE MILITARY HISTORY AND MARINE LIFE MEET

The *Antilla* is one of the most coveted dive sites in the Caribbean. At 121.4m in length, this cargo ship is the sea's third-largest submerged wreck. Well, *mostly* submerged; part of the starboard hull sticks out of the water, while most of it rests diagonally against the seafloor.

Left Seascape, *Antilla* wreck
Center *Pedernales* wreck
Right *Antilla* wreck and diver

DARYL DUDA/SHUTTERSTOCK

Part of the appeal of the **Antilla** is its proximity to the shore: the site is only 550m from Boca Catalina Beach, which is too far to swim but easy to access by boat. Divers can hang around the shallower parts or swim down to the deepest points, 18m below the surface. But, how did such a leviathan get here? Unlike so many other wrecks along the Aruban coast, the *Antilla* wasn't sunk for the sake of reef-building, and the last thing authorities wanted was to lose this particular vessel to the sea. The story of the *Antilla* is one of war, sabotage and a remarkable reincarnation as one of Aruba's hottest attractions.

A WWII Saga

By the late 1930s, Aruba maintained two of the world's largest oil refineries, which would become vital resources as the Netherlands was dragged into WWII. The Dutch anticipated that Aruba's facilities and cargo ships would be vulnerable to attack and helped establish a blockade against German vessels.

At the same time, the SS *Antilla* was a brand-new German merchant ship sailing its way through the Caribbean. In January of 1940, fearing that Allied forces might commandeer the *Antilla*, the ship's captain dropped anchor off of the northwest coast of Aruba, which was then considered a safe, neutral port. There it stayed for four months, both island and ship stuck in a geopolitical stalemate.

On May 11, Dutch marines were finally ordered to board the *Antilla*. To prevent its capture, the *Antilla*'s crew stealthily opened the seacocks – hatches that admit

DARYL DUDA/SHUTTERSTOCK

GUSTAVOQUIROGA/SHUTTERSTOCK

water – and started fires as well. The ship began to sink, vomiting smoke and listing to one side.

The crew all survived as prisoners of war, and its cargo never reached Axis ports. But the scuttled ship was a loss for the Dutch, who might have otherwise used it in the war effort. This bloodless event was a foreboding overture to more violent encounters; enemy ships would continue to play cat-and-mouse in the Caribbean for the next five years, including a full-blown U-boat assault on Aruba in 1942, which would result in six tankers sunk and about 50 hands lost.

> The story of the *Antilla* is one of war, sabotage and a remarkable reincarnation as one of Aruba's hottest attractions.

Underwater Revival

Since that fateful day, the *Antilla* has broken into two pieces, which are each covered in fuzzy blankets of coral and tube sponges. The corroded bridge and gunwales retain much of their original shape, making homes for lobsters, anemones and brightly patterned fish. The site attracts divers of all abilities, who can explore this strange monument – and take heart that no ghosts haunt its abraded decks.

The sinking of the *Antilla* represents a bleak chapter in the Caribbean's history, when the future of the free world hung in the balance. But like so many places on this island, Arubans have given this monument a new purpose, where life begins anew.

⚓ The Pedernales

One of Aruba's strangest wrecks is the **SS *Pedernales***, a tanker that was also targeted during WWII.

As a dive site, the *Pedernales* remains largely intact, but it may seem like something is missing. The reason? When U-boats damaged the ship in 1942, the Dutch cut off the bow and stern, which were salvaged into a new ship. The middle section was used for target practice, until it was finally released to the depths off of the northwest coast, where it remains a popular relic.

Lying 10m below the surface, it's an ideal spot for scuba novices.

Listings

BEST OF THE REST

Hidden Restaurants

Saliña Local Cuisine $

First feast on burgers, shrimp sandwiches and whole fish, then cool off in the on-site pool at this easygoing outdoor restaurant. Tables for two are positioned under *palapas*, and colorful cocktails can be sipped in the water. Located in the Esmeralda Westpunt development, it's perfect for a post-Malmok dinner.

Faro Blanco Restaurant $$$

Elegant Italian restaurant, steps from the California Lighthouse and overlooking the Tierra del Sol golf course. The northernmost fine-dining establishment in Aruba prepares decadent fish and lobster platters alongside comprehensive wine pairings. The sunset views and masterful cuisine make this one of the country's best dining experiences.

Restaurant at Tierra del Sol $$$

There's no better way to end an afternoon on the course (or at the spa) than at a well-stocked bar. Oh, wait, maybe add a dynamic tapas menu as well. Tierra del Sol's flagship restaurant serves gorgeous plates of halibut and short rib, plus raw-bar classics.

Ocean Z $$$

Ocean Z is a five-star boutique hotel, located next to Malmok Beach. Even if you're not staying in its luxury suites, you can enjoy dinner in Ocean Z's acclaimed restaurant. The Mediterranean-infused menu includes outstanding seafood paella and *linguine di frutti di mare* (seafood pasta).

Arashi Beach Shack $$

Waffles, crab sandwiches and shrimp skewers – this place has it all. Tucked into the north side of Arashi Beach, this place is your number-one snack bar. Enjoy drinks on the terrace, and even organize a diving or dune buggy tour inside the shack.

Northern Hotspots

Boroncana Post di Noord Trail

At the end of Boroncana Rd, on the edge of a residential development, you'll find a dirt track that disappears into the rocks and cactuses. This short hike takes you to the top of Sero Pela, a secluded hill with decent views, before splitting off in several directions.

Urirama Beach

The northeast coast of Aruba is a quilt of contrasting surfaces, and Urirama Beach has them all, from pumice stones to ragged rock faces to silky sands. The dusty main road skirts the edge of this beach, making it a natural pit-stop for drivers, hikers or ATVers.

STBAR1964/SHUTTERSTOCK

Arashi Beach Shack

Elisa Lejuez Art

Long before Elisa Lejuez opened her art gallery in Aruba's Noord, she studied fine art in the Netherlands and worked in the textile industry. The gallery showcases Lejuez's colorful, pop-infused paintings and scarves. Long-term visitors can also sign up for art classes on site.

Banana Adventure

Headquartered a few blocks away from busy Fisherman's Hut, Banana Adventure is a tour company that can organize just about anything: catamarans, kayaks, a bar-hopping bus and, most striking of all, the *Seabob* mini-submarine, which efficiently guides free-divers into lower depths.

EWY MEDIA/SHUTTERSTOCK

Banana Adventure bus

More Undersea Wrecks

Debbie II

The 40m-long tanker *Debbie II* has rested off the northwest coast since 1991, accumulating a diverse array of coral and fish. The ship stands next to Blue Reef, about 21m below the surface, a depth best suited to intermediate divers.

California

A century after its sinking, chunks of the SS *California* are shockingly well preserved off the northernmost coast of Aruba. Don't let the 13m depth deceive you: these waters are subject to strong currents and only seasoned divers should take them on.

Star Gerren

Intermediate divers will love this 69m-long coaster lying about 3km west of Palm Beach. Broken and lying almost upside-down at a depth of about 30m, the *Star Gerren* remains mostly intact, and large passages allow you to swim inside the ship as well.

Jane C

According to legend, the *Jane C* was a freighter that transported cement across the Atlantic – until contraband was discovered in her hold. The tarnished ship was eventually sunk in 1988 off the western coast of Savaneta, and today the *Jane C* is caked in sea life at 18m below the surface.

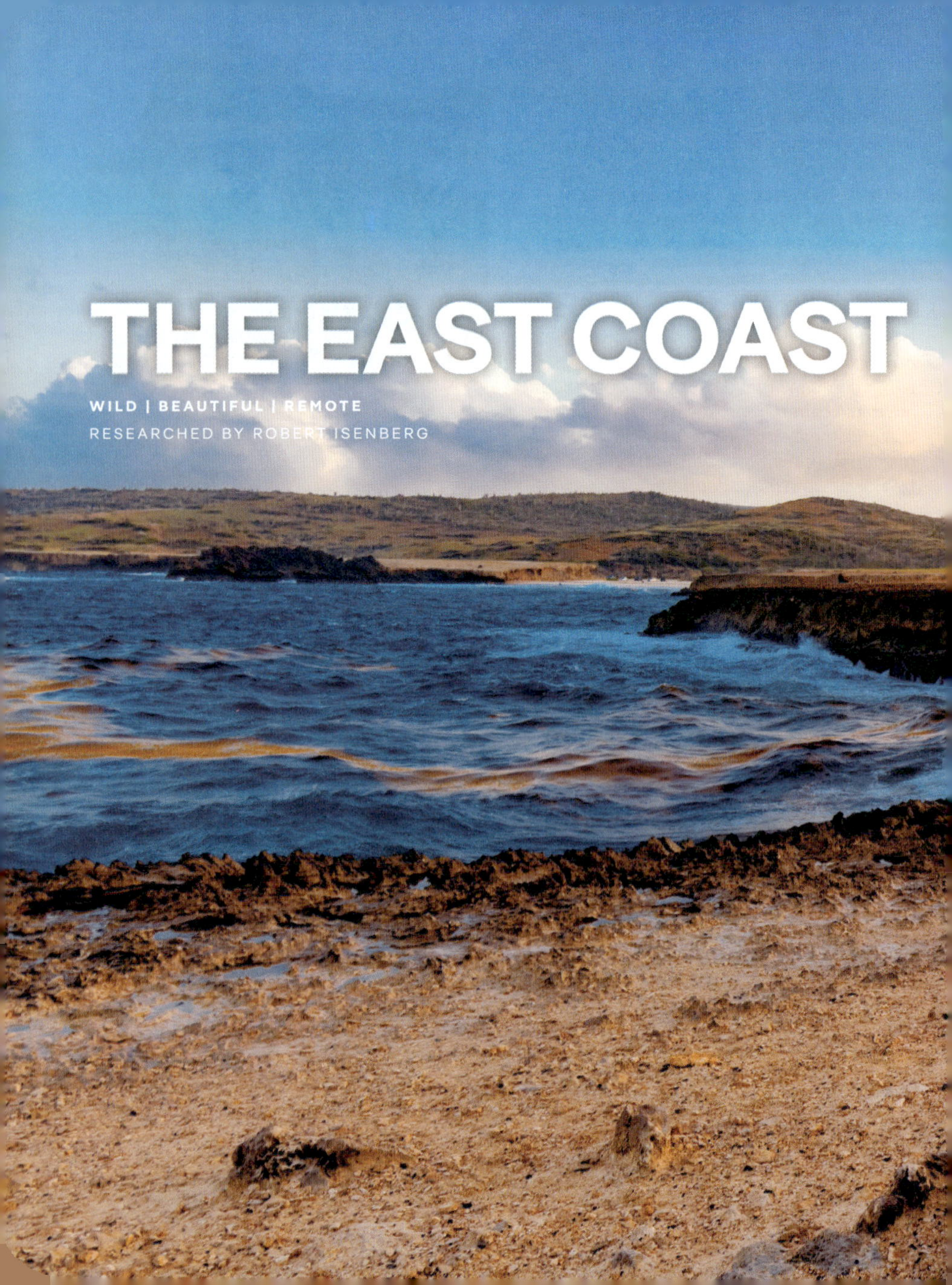

THE EAST COAST

WILD | BEAUTIFUL | REMOTE

RESEARCHED BY ROBERT ISENBERG

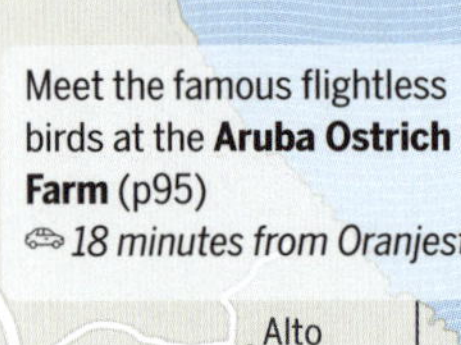

Meet the famous flightless birds at the **Aruba Ostrich Farm** (p95)
18 minutes from Oranjestad

0 — 2 km
0 — 1 mile

Alto Vista

Noord

Caribbean Sea

Poke around mysterious boulders at the **Ayo Rock Formations** (p99)
15 minutes from Oranjestad

Ayo

Dive from the rock-hewn rim of **Conchi Natural Pool** (p102)
30 minutes from Oranjestad

Oranjestad

Cas Ariba

Santa Cruz

Arikok National Park

Climb to the top of Aruba's second-tallest mountain, **Hooiberg** (p99)
12 minutes from Oranjestad

Mt Jamanota

Slip inside the limestone halls of the **Quadirikiri Cave** (p101)
40 minutes from Oranjestad

EAST COAST
Trip Builder

The east coast is Aruba's cactus-studded frontier, a world apart from the bustle of Oranjestad and unsullied by human development. Here, the island's natural beauty comes into focus. Enter a primal land of cliffs, caves and crashing surf.

FROM LEFT: FRANCOIS GAGNON/SHUTTERSTOCK, ULTIMA_GAINA/GETTY IMAGES
PREVIOUS SPREAD: DIEGOMARIOTTINI/SHUTTERSTOCK

Practicalities

MONEY

When you enter Arikok National Park at the visitor center near San Fuego, you can pay with credit card or cash.

ARRIVING

There's no bus service here, but the east coast is what rental cars were made for. Road-trippers will find curving backroads and photogenic vistas.

FIND YOUR WAY

The easiest drive along the east coast is to take Rte 7 from Oranjestad to the water. Note that the narrow highway reverts to dirt.

WHERE TO STAY

City/Area	Pros/Cons
Resort District	Lots of comfy accommodations, and tours are easily arranged. Further from Arikok National Park.
Oranjestad	Closer to the park, with budget hotels. City traffic may slow you down.
Savaneta	Lots of hotel options, off the beaten track; use the Vader Piet entrance to Arikok Park.

GETTING AROUND

Car A rental is the easiest way to hop along the east coast. Taxis will take you out here, but they're harder to flag down for the return trip, and Aruba has no rideshare program.

On foot The east coast is a hiker's paradise, thanks to rugged trails and rocky surfaces to scramble over. Do bring food, water and sunscreen.

TOP AND BOTTOM: STUDIO MURANO ART RESTAURANT

EATING & DRINKING

The east coast is sparsely developed, and even the most basic amenities are scattered across a desert landscape. Before you head out this way, pack food and fresh water.

The closest restaurants to the shore are at least 15 minutes west by car.

Best pit-stop Urataka Center (p107)

Must-try experience Restaurant Murano Art (p107; pictured top and bottom left)

ALL YEAR
The east coast is dry, breezy and comparatively low-traffic most months of the year.

FEB & MAR
Head to remote beaches to escape the Carnival crowds.

SEP–NOV
A little overcast can be a blessing in these hot climes.

13 Wonders of THE EAST

ANIMALS | NATURE | ADVENTURE

Ostriches, horses, natural pools – north of Arikok National Park, you'll find an appealing line of natural wonders. You would never guess that this quiet corner of Aruba offers so many diversions, and it's hard to believe, standing in rural settings on the opposite side of the country, that you're (at most) a 25-minute drive from downtown Oranjestad.

ULTIMA_GAINA/GETTY IMAGES

Trip Notes

Getting here and around: You'll probably have to take a motor vehicle, whether taxi or rental car. Conveniently, all these destinations stand in a row. You can also reach them on bikes or ATVs.

When to go: All of these attractions are open during the day only.

Footwear: You're wise to bring durable shoes or hiking boots as well as sandals.

Coastal Escape

I love starting my day with an early-morning hike in **Arikok National Park**. After a hot, busy day, I head to **Boca Catalina** for a sunset dip. On weekends, you'll find me at **LIMA Bistro** enjoying the freshest and most creative ceviche.

Edeline Berg *is the communications manager at the Aruba Conservation Foundation (ACF)*

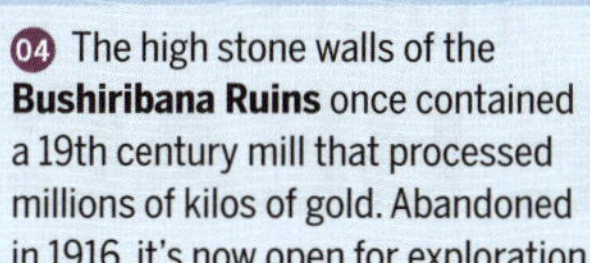

04 The high stone walls of the **Bushiribana Ruins** once contained a 19th century mill that processed millions of kilos of gold. Abandoned in 1916, it's now open for exploration.

02 Mount a horse and ride down to the beach at the **Gold Mine Ranch** (thegoldmineranch.com), a stable and tour operator that offers beach rides, multi-modal safaris and cantering along the sand.

03 Tucked beneath a slanted rock wall is the **Cave Pool**. These clear waters are just deep enough to jump into feet-first, and overhanging stone keeps you shaded. The best part: it's free.

01 Flock to the **Aruba Ostrich Farm** (aruba ostrichfarm.com) to see 18 ostriches, 16 emus and scores of other avians up close. Join an hourly guided tour to learn about these African transplants.

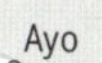

05 The massive slab that forms the **Natural Bridge** is about 30m long. The original coral bridge collapsed in 2004, leaving this smaller one. It's still photogenic, but walking across it is prohibited.

FROM TOP: ERIK ALVARADO/ALAMY, PHOTOSHOPAV/SHUTTERSTOCK

14 Lose Yourself on THE BEACH

PRIVACY | WAVES | GEOLOGY

Wedged into a wall of shallow cliffs, Andicuri Beach is a peaceful rectangle of sand that is caressed all day by powerful waves. The beach is small and quiet, except for the whistle of wind and sizzle of water. Come here for peace and solitude – and maybe some bodysurfing. Afterward, scope out the nearby natural marvels.

YINGNA CAI/SHUTTERSTOCK

How to

Getting here and around: The direct roads to Andicuri are rough and dusty, and only a 4WD or ATV will make the trip unscathed. Easier on the axle is parking at the Tripod Bridge and walking 15 minutes along the coastal trail.

When to go: Andicuri is beautiful year-round. The strength of the waves changes with the tides.

Go before you go: There are no restrooms in or around Andicuri.

SERGE YATUNIN/SHUTTERSTOCK

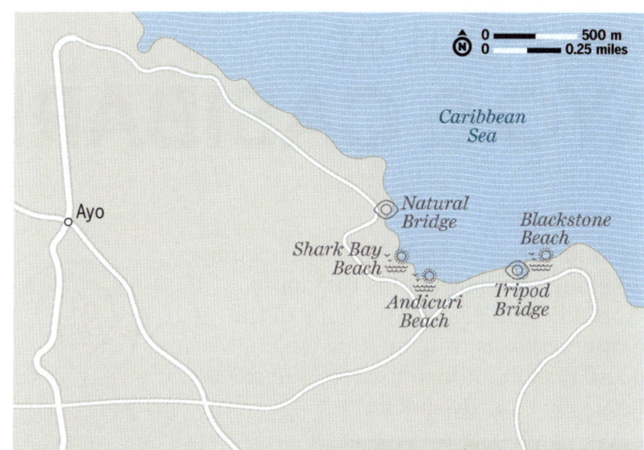

Far left top Andicuri Beach
Far left bottom Blackstone Beach

Ride the waves Unlike the tranquil waters of Aruba's west coast, the sea around **Andicuri Beach** is consistently choppy. You won't find a lot of full-on surfing here, perhaps because it's a challenge to get to or because surfers worry about the beach's rocky bookends. Still, this is a fantastic place to bob in the water or bring a small boogie board; just be careful around Andicuri's robust undertow. This is also a peaceful little setting to catch some rays or enjoy a picnic.

Tread the black stones Stroll over to **Blackstone Beach**, about 15 minutes away on foot, smelling salty Caribbean air as you inch around Andicuri Bay. Blackstone is named for its dark, pebbled surface and the smoky-looking rock formations all around. This tinted appearance is unique in Aruba. The beach's stones are worn smooth, and the scenery is ripe for photos, but the waters aren't convenient for swimming, and you're wise to wear shoes around the sharp crags.

Tough trio The east coast is famous for its 'natural bridges,' stone arcs that hover boldly over the crashing water. Right next to Blackstone Beach is the **Tripod Bridge**, which joins three of these spans together. You're welcome to cross them on foot and snap a picture; they extend just a couple of meters from the coastal road.

Shark Bay Beach

If the tranquility of Andicuri still isn't private enough, you can venture just 10 minutes further down the footpaths to **Shark Bay Beach**. Here the cliffs form a kind of protective awning over the sand and water. Shark Bay is a subtle little inlet, but these waters are noticeably calmer than Andicuri and yield an astonishing range of marine species, including the occasional shark. Bring the snorkel and a waterproof camera, as you're bound to find colorful fish flitting among the waves.

Since you've come this far anyway, you may continue down the path to the **Natural Bridge**, 20 minutes north on foot.

15 Rock Out at AYO & CASIBARI

ROCK FORMATIONS | LOOKOUTS | HIKING

Become one with the land. Some of Aruba's most arresting landscapes are composed of stone, and nowhere is that more evident than in the island's middle and east coast. Many of the more picturesque sites are interactive as well, inviting agile visitors to climb, scramble and explore hidden fissures. There's no need to bring ropes or helmets, just sturdy shoes.

STBARI1964/SHUTTERSTOCK

How to

Getting here and around: Ayo and Casibari are both located in Oranjestad's eastern suburbs, and they're each about 8km from downtown, which translates to 15 minutes by car and 30 minutes by bicycle.

When to go: Mornings are best, before the rocky surfaces start to bake in the midday heat. The sunset views are also stunning from their tops.

Bring the binoculars: These horizons demand telescopic viewing.

NENAD BASIC/SHUTTERSTOCK

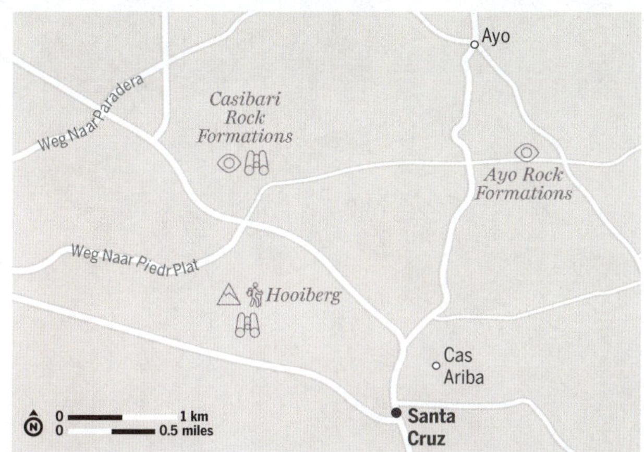

Far left top Casibari Rock Formations
Far left bottom Hooiberg peak

Natural view When you see the **Casibari Rock Formations** from a distance, they almost look like a single stone dome. Only when you get closer do you see how this dome has fragmented into giant wedges of tonalite. The Arawak people were said to come to Casibari to watch for coming thunderstorms, and traces of petroglyphs are still etched into the sandpaper-like walls. A modern staircase leads to the top of Casibari; the steps take only a minute or two to ascend, and a guardrail cordons off a de facto terrace. Savor a 360-degree view of residential neighborhoods, as well as Hooiberg looming in the middle distance.

Great mound The **Ayo Rock Formations** are similar to Casibari, and attract the same kinds of hikers and history buffs. Like Casibari, the Ayo site was likely formed millions of years ago by shifting tectonic plates; this process began deep underwater and only gradually did the formation rise to the surface. Unlike its sibling, Ayo is a pile of rounded boulders, like a gigantic cairn, and many visitors liken the shapes of the rocks to animals. The terrain here is more dynamic and the cobblestone trail a little longer than at Casibari; expect to spend at least 20 minutes making your way to the top and back. The crags are rich in local plantlife, and if you're lucky, you'll spot a resident goat among the bluffs.

Hoof up Hooiberg

There's no missing **Hooiberg**: the 165m-tall mountain rises abruptly out of the flats, marking the geographic center of the island. While it's not exactly on the 'east coast,' Hooiberg shares the raw topography of that sparsely populated region, its slopes scruffy with rocks and bushes.

Like Ayo and Casibari, Hooiberg boasts a single stairway that ascends from foot to summit. This climb will get the blood flowing, and hydration is vital. Still, most visitors should reach the top, a rock patch crowned with radio towers. Your reward: the best view in Aruba, and a much easier walk down.

16 Adventures on the WILD SIDE

NATURE | BEAUTY | EXERCISE

Arikok National Park dominates Aruba's east coast – and one-fifth of the entire island – with 32 sq km of protected land. You could spend days exploring this wild country by car, on foot or in a saddle.

SERGE YATUNIN/SHUTTERSTOCK

How to

Getting here and around: Visiting Arikok requires a motor vehicle, but this can take the form of rental car, taxi, scooter or UTV.

When to go: Mornings are best, especially in the drier months (February to April), before the sun gets high.

Park fee: Entrance is US$22 per adult; guests age 17 and under are free.

SABINE_LJ/SHUTTERSTOCK

Explore the Caves

Quadirikiri Cave looks like the set of a fantasy movie: the textured ceiling is vaulted with rock and openings in the top behave like skylights, shooting blades of light into the cool darkness. The two dome-shaped chambers are easy to enter on your own, and park rangers posted outside regularly give free tours. A handy staircase leads into Quadirikiri, and the cave isn't very deep, but be aware that this site is not wheelchair accessible.

Just 2.5km along the dirt highway lies **Fontein Cave**. While this little grotto is shallower than Quadirikiri and has a lower ceiling, Fontein boasts several massive stalactites that extend from floor to ceiling, like primordial pillars. Decorative rocks have also been laid out on the cave floor, giving the space a

DAVID G HAYES/SHUTTERSTOCK

Hello & Goodbye

Faced with so much open land, you might wonder where the campgrounds are. Actually, there isn't a single campsite or RV hookup anywhere in Aruba, let alone Arikok. The park is open from 8am to 4pm only; make the most of daylight hours, and plan to stay under a regular roof.

Far left top Quadirikiri Cave
Far left bottom Fontein Cave entrance
Above Dos Playa (p102)

delicate human touch. If you've already paid to enter Arikok National Park, both caves are free to visit and open to the public 8am to 4pm. Each is located right off Rte 7; note that nearby Huliba Cave is closed for the foreseeable future, in an effort to protect resident bat populations.

Dos Playa

The two sandy strips of **Dos Playa** lie right next to each other, separated by a rocky shelf. Like Andicuri Beach, these twins are powdery, remote and famous for their waves. If you love to hike, the journey is just as fun as the destination: visitors should park (or get dropped off) at the **Arikok Visitor Center**, right near the San Fuego entrance. The trail makes an 8km loop through rocky savanna; budget a little over two hours for the hike, then more time to bask in the sea. Bring all necessary provisions with you, as this route doesn't have a single store or service.

Conchi Natural Pool

Seeing the **Conchi Natural Pool**, you may not believe your eyes: this oblong body of water is rimmed with cliffs, and the 5m depth is just right for diving and cannonballs. Waves smash against the rocky barrier, sending geysers of spray over swimmers.

Conchi couldn't be more perfect if an engineer had designed it, yet the pool was shaped naturally over eons. ('Conchi' is the Papiamento word for 'bowl').

A rutted access road leads to a dirt parking lot, followed by a rubbled 10-minute hike to the pool. Admission is free with park entry.

Left Conchi Natural Pool
Below Horses, Aruba

Bridle Paths

Believe it or not, horse-trading played a major role in Aruba's economy for centuries, and one of the best ways to explore the pitted trails of Arikok is still atop a saddle. Rural Aruba looks a lot like the Old West, and the equestrian guides of **Rancho Loco** (rancholocoaruba.com) can't wait to show you the bridle paths that wend between the cactuses.

Riders should be at least eight years old and weigh 100kg or less; otherwise, no experience is required. Horses trot at a leisurely pace down the Nacho Trail, which eventually leads to Moro Beach and the Conchi Natural Pool.

For US$140, riders explore Arikok's dynamic lowlands, cool off in the water, then make their way back, all in the span of 2½ hours.

FROM LEFT: BY MARC GUITARD/GETTY IMAGES, ALLANSANEDRIN/GETTY IMAGES

EAST COAST
Flora, Fauna & Landscapes

01 Petroglyph
Like many Indigenous groups, the Arawaks drew figures on rock faces. Some petroglyphs still remain at the Casibari Rock Formations.

02 Breba Cactus
This long-armed cactus is the tallest succulent in Aruba.

03 Long-Haired Goat
Many transplanted goats now roam freely in the Aruban hills. You may spot them around the Ayo Rock Formations.

04 Aruba Whiptail
Endemic to the island, these tongue-flicking lizards come in many different colors. They're a common sight – and totally harmless.

05 Natural Bridge
This stone span is one of the most famous images in the country. You can't walk across it, but it makes for a dramatic photo.

07

06

09

08

10

06 Prikichi
This lime-green parakeet is native to Aruba. You can sometimes spot the official national bird perched in branches.

07 Ostrich
Yes, ostriches live in Africa, but they also feature prominently at the Aruba Ostrich Farm, along with emus.

08 Horse
Aruba was once an outpost for horse traders. While ATVs are useful in the back-country, horses are still masters of the trails.

09 Black Stone
Aruba's smooth dark rocks exist only at Blackstone Beach, where even the cliffs have been mysteriously stained a dark shade.

10 Aloe Plant
The famous healing plant grows wild – and big – in Aruba's outback. Cultivating aloe is a big part of the economy.

01 DAVID G HAYES/SHUTTERSTOCK, **02** BLUEORANGE STUDIO/SHUTTERSTOCK, **03** AVIV JOSHUA/GETTY IMAGES, **04** LISA A ERNST/SHUTTERSTOCK, **05** FSENDEK/SHUTTERSTOCK, **06** FRANK DE GROENE/GETTY IMAGES, **07** MRALI00/SHUTTERSTOCK, **08** ZAWARM356/SHUTTERSTOCK, **09** JONATHAN BOXWELL/SHUTTERSTOCK, **10** REDHELGA/GETTY IMAGES

Listings

BEST OF THE REST

Trails

Daimari Beach

This private beach was formerly the setting for Aruba Rancho Daimari. Nowadays, hikers start near the defunct horse ranch and thread their way over the hills, toward the Conchi Natural Pool. There and back is about 4.5km.

Mt Jamanota

'Jamanota' refers to several things, all of which are connected: there's the access road, which is gated off at a parking area; there's Jamanota Trail, a 3km loop up the rugged escarpment; and then there's Jamanota Hill, a modest rise in Arikok's terrain with splendid views of the park.

Arikok Mountain

From the San Fuego entrance, take a left along winding dirt roads. Arikok Mountain stands only 100m or so above sea level, but you'll get a decent view of the cactus-studded landscape – and maybe spot a goat or two.

Butucu Trail

Park at Fontein Cave and hike directly south, where you'll find trails that ascend the scrub-coated slopes. This 3km route will lead you up to Butucu, a stretch of uninhabited foothills and erstwhile archaeological site. Make sure to bring water; this is Aruba's truest wilderness.

Coastal Spots

Wariruri Beach

Driving out to this obscure corner of the east coast will reward surfers with impressive waves and lots of privacy. Wariruri Bay is just a five-minute drive from the Bushiribana Ruins, but layers of tall cactus and cliff make it feel completely cut off.

Lince's Cove

Also known as Boca Mahos, Lince's Cove is like a lot of inlets along the east coast, with its cliffs, waves and modest triangle of sand. If you're over here and need some sea, the cove is only 400m from the Cave Pool.

Boca Keto

This little cove has several attractions. First, the White Dunes, a soft stretch of sand just south of Daimiri Beach. Then, once you reach the water, you'll spot Klein Aruba, a massive table of rock topped with grass. Klein Aruba itself is off-limits, but you can snorkel all around it.

Boca Putri

A 10-minute hike down the coast from the Conchi Natural Pool, Boca Putri is a seldom-visited cove rimmed with dark rocks. The views are pleasant, and the waves crash dramatically against a dynamic shore.

PHOTOSHOPAV/SHUTTERSTOCK

Chapel of Alto Vista

Boca Prins

Named after the family – and plantation – that once stood nearby, Boca Prins is a wave-battered little beach hemmed in by cliffs. Stairs lead down to silky sands, and the views of the sea are beautiful to behold. The entrance is just a five-minute walk from Fontein Cave.

Manmade Curiosities

Chapel of Alto Vista

With its bright-yellow walls, tiny steeple and medieval-looking wood doors, Alto Vista Chapel is a picturesque Catholic shrine in Aruba's northeastern corner. Completed in 1952, it has a handful of pews and a modest altar. Outside, the cactus-studded hill overlooks the sea.

Vader Piet Wind Farm

It's impossible to miss the massive white turbines of the southeastern coast, especially on a windy day, when the Vader Piet blades busily rotate. These machines have generated about 15% of Aruba's electricity since they were first erected in 2009.

Urataka Center

The last big restaurant you'll pass before you reach Arikok National Park is this mission-style roadhouse, with its corrugated-steel roof and brightly painted balustrades.

IGAL SHKOLNIK/SHUTTERSTOCK

Lince's Cove

Enjoy pizza and wings during the day, then beer and live music come nightfall.

Restaurant Murano Art

Owner Giuliano Pinzan demonstrates his glass-blowing skills for the public (daily, 10am to 1pm) and also leads classes in this ancient art form. Studio Murano triples as a store for original glass items as well as scrumptious restaurant and bar. Browse gifts, then enjoy some burgers, pizzas and beer.

Plantage Prins

Plantage Prins is the long-abandoned country house of a century-old coconut plantation. The roof has long collapsed and all that remains are walls, but the haunting ruin hints at Aruba's history and makes for striking photos.

SAN NICOLAS & THE SOUTH COAST

RAW | AUTHENTIC | ARTISTIC

RESEARCHED BY ROBERT ISENBERG

0 2 km
0 1 mile

Caribbean Sea

Cas Ariba

Santa Cruz

Pet animals and learn about equine history at **Donkey Sanctuary** (p121)
25 minutes from San Nicolas

Mt Jamanota

Arikok National Park

De Palm Island

Paddle a kayak into the mangroves of **Spanish Lagoon** (p116)
20 minutes from San Nicolas

Savaneta

San Nicolas

Browse the work of San Nicolas' groundbreaking artists at **ArtisA** (p114)
1 minute from San Nicolas traffic circle

Drink and catch some local singers at legendary **Charlie's Bar** (p123)
5 minutes from San Nicolas traffic circle

SOUTH COAST

Trip Builder

Oil refineries and close-knit neighborhoods. Diverse residents and prolific artists. If there is a 'real Aruba,' you'll find it in the south. Historic and low-key, these working-class communities are pillars of local culture.

Wade in warm waters and sun with locals at **Baby Beach** (p112)
15 minutes from downtown San Nicolas

FROM LEFT: KITTIPONG KONGWATMAI/SHUTTERSTOCK, GLOBE GUIDE MEDIA INC/SHUTTERSTOCK
PREVIOUS SPREAD: DERSON SANTANA/SHUTTERSTOCK

Practicalities

MONEY

Most established businesses should accept credit cards, but cash is more popular in the south, especially among smaller merchants.

ARRIVING

Queen Beatrix International Airport Everyone flies into Oranjestad. From there, a car, taxi or bus will get you to San Nicolas – any hotel down here is at most a 20-minute drive.

FIND YOUR WAY

The center of San Nicolas is a commercial corridor called Zeppenfeldstraat. The **San Nicolas Visitor Center** stands across from the central roundabout.

WHERE TO STAY

Town/Area	Pros/Cons
Downtown San Nicolas	Full of food, drink and entertainment; can get loud at night.
Savaneta	A pleasant small town with lots to do; fewer fellow travelers.
Baby Beach	A favorite local beach; far from tourist amenities.

GETTING AROUND

Car A rental car is handy in these spread-out suburbs. Cabs are easy to find in town centers.

Bus Several public bus routes run through San Nicolas.

Walking Downtown San Nicolas and Savaneta are walkable, with dining and nightlife within a few blocks of hotels.

TOP: MARTIN RETTENBERGER/SHUTTERSTOCK
BOTTOM: GOSS IMAGES/ALAMY

EATING & DRINKING

Far from the upscale restaurants of the resort area, southern restaurants tend to serve local favorites, like *stabo* (a classic beef stew) and *funchi* (Aruba's answer to polenta; pictured top left). Bars around here offer their share of fancy cocktails, but you're more likely to see buckets of Balashi (pictured bottom left), Aruba's national beer.

Best Bar Charlie's Bar (p123)

Must-try dining Old Man and the Sea Restaurant (p126)

BUSY SEASONS
Laid-back San Nicolas peaks around two major events.

JAN–MAR
Carnival is an island-wide affair, with a massive Grand Parade in San Nicolas.

SEP & OCT
The Aruba Art Fair takes place in September; October travel beats the holiday rush.

17 San Nicolas BEACH LIFE

QUIET | LOCALS | FOOD

Life is chill on the San Nicolas coast. Head down here for vast beaches, home-style restaurants and under-the-radar natural landscapes. These easygoing shores lie only 30km from Aruba's resort area, yet they feel like another planet, where tourists are few and far between and local parents picnic with their children. Spend a day falling into San Nicolas' soothing rhythm.

How to

Getting around: Most visitors drive to Baby Beach, where you'll find a free parking lot; other destinations are best reached by car. Cycling is less common, but very possible.

When to go: These beaches are sublime any time of day, but Baby Beach is technically open from 8am to 8pm.

Rent elsewhere: These waters are ideal for stand-up paddleboarding, but there are no on-site shops that rent boards.

0 500 m
0 0.25 miles
Grapefield Beach
Caribbean Sea
Seroe Colorado Natural Bridge
Stairs to the Sea
Rodger's Beach
Baby Beach
Rum Reef
Big Mama Grill

Hey, Baby

If you ask locals their favorite place to play in the water, they're almost certain to say **Baby Beach**. Tucked into the southernmost tip of Aruba, this dreamy little cove has plush sand, bath-like water and a family-friendly vibe. The scenery is a bit less glamorous than in the north; you can spot refinery towers in the distance, and the local penitentiary is just down the road. Yet Baby Beach is a great place to interact with actual Arubans and snorkel in shallow waters.

Once you've burned some calories in the sea, grab lunch at the **Rum Reef** (rumreef aruba.com) cocktail bar or Afro-Caribbean-style **Big Mama Grill** (big mamagrillaruba.com).

Step This Way

Right next door, **Rodger's Beach** plays second fiddle to Baby Beach, but it does boast a delightful landmark: the **Stairs to the Sea**, a

ORIETTA GASPARI/GETTY IMAGES

multi-tiered walkway with hand-painted steps. Rodger's Beach is less popular with tourists, but you'll likely spot fishers dragging their boats onto the floury shore.

East Coast Solitude

As you drive from San Nicolas toward Arikok National Park, you'll pass a long, sandy coast with little development and few people.

The main attraction here is **Grapefield Beach**, a little-known launchpad for kiteboarders and a decent place to dip your toes in the sea. You may see as many wild goats as humans on this understated stretch.

Seroe Colorado Natural Bridge

One of the most magical sights in Aruba is the **Seroe Colorado Natural Bridge**, a perfect shaft of limestone that arcs over rocks and tidepools to the east of Baby Beach. Nearly 5m high at its apex, Seroe Colorado is narrower and more attractive than the Natural Bridge of Arikok National Park, yet its obscure location means far fewer visitors.

Walking across the bridge is prohibited, and fans worry that this sedimentary monument will one day collapse, but the photographs alone are worth the short, craggy hike here.

Above Rodger's Beach

18 Tour the ART

PUBLIC | CREATIVITY | GIFTS

Who would have guessed a nation of 107,000 people had so many fine artists? Take a good walk around San Nicolas and count how many works of art you see, painted on walls, hanging in galleries and decorating local establishments. Observe how creative residents have beautified their city – and maybe take home some of their gorgeous handiwork.

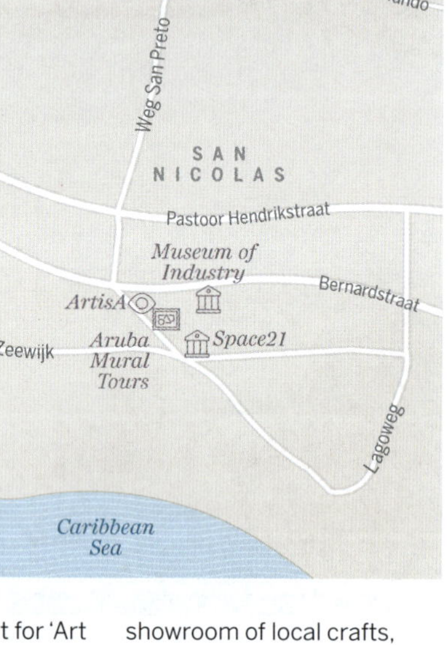

How to

Getting around: San Nicolas' galleries and public murals are clustered around Zeppenfeldstraat, making them easiest to visit on foot.

When to go: Galleries are open around traditional business hours; the annual Aruba Art Fair takes place in September.

Luggage-ready: Many items for sale are sized for carry-on luggage.

Art galleries The middle of old San Nicolas has become Aruba's arts district, where several prominent galleries show local work.

The linchpin of this scene is **ArtisA** (artisaruba.com), a showspace and community center just three blocks northwest of the central traffic circle. Founded by social entrepreneur Tito Bolivar, ArtisA is short for 'Art is Aruba,' and the institution takes this slogan to heart: the San Nicolas public murals and Aruba Art Fair are both spearheaded by ArtisA. The building is always busy with exhibits and workshops, and patrons can drop in anytime from 9am to 5pm.

Nearby galleries include **Space21** (space21.art), a showroom of local crafts, jewelry and fashion, and the **Aruflamingo Art Cafe** (aruflamingo-art.com), a coffeehouse packed with Caribbean-themed paintings and sculpture.

Mural tours In 2016, the first public murals went up in San Nicolas, turning this old industrial community into a citywide art gallery. Visitors

YINGNA CAI/SHUTTERSTOCK

are often shocked at what they find: photo-realistic portraits of human faces, a carnival dancer, a lionfish and a hummingbird, among countless other images.

One mural is a 3D sculpture of a crab, crafted out of repurposed rubbishTo learn the backstory of these 50-odd works, sign up for the **Aruba Mural Tours** (arubamuraltours.com).

Celebrate arts Each September, the week-long **Aruba Art Fair** (arubaartfair.com) draws international artists and over 12,000 attendees. Booths line the streets, collectors browse original works and concerts and food vendors take over public spaces.

Museum of Industry

Believe it or not, that cylindrical building in the middle of town was once a water-tower, and today its 1st floor doubles as the **Museum of Industry**. This smartly curated exhibition was first opened in 2016 to illustrate Aruba's history of gold mining and oil refineries.

Archival photographs and period artifacts reveal the evolving landscape of Aruba's economy, as workers dug up the soil and pumped petrol into freighter ships, leaving lasting impressions on San Nicolas in particular.

Housed in the beautifully restored art deco tower, the museum is open Monday to Friday mornings and costs US$5 per visitor.

Above Hymn to the Sea mural, San Nicolas

19 Explore Spanish LAGOON

KAYAKS | MANGROVES | HIKING

In a country that receives less than 50cm of rain each year, Spanish Lagoon is a refreshing change of scenery: a coastal bay that is a lush wetland and wildlife habitat. To see this area up close, paddle down the channels in a kayak, hike the surrounding trails or while away some hours on the adjacent beach.

How to

Getting around: By car, Rte 1 will take you right to the edge of Spanish Lagoon, where you'll find free parking. After that, explore the reserve on foot. Kayakers will paddle in from the southern coast.

When to go: The rainy season (October to January) is the best time to visit, as the foliage will be greenest.

Insect repellent: Mosquitoes aren't a major concern in Aruba, but they do breed in these still waters.

Kayak the Mangroves

These dark waters and bushy shores contrast sharply with the Aruban coast, making it a super place on the island to paddle a kayak or SUP. For US$80 per person, sign up for a two-hour tour with **Aruba Outdoor Adventures** (arubaoutdooradventures.com), which will provide all equipment and a naturalist guide. The office is conveniently located at the mouth of the bay.

Hike Around the Lagoon

Level dirt trails encircle the lagoon, which make for easy hiking through this leafy sanctuary. It's free to visit and explore on your own, or you can join a three-hour hike and birdwatching trip with **Aruba Nature Adventures** (arubaeco.tours). Spot wildlife, learn the history of the area and hear the ghost story behind Haunted Frenchman's Pass. As a bonus, you'll get photogenic views of the nearby suspension bridge.

FLAVIO VALLENARI/GETTY IMAGES

Hidden in Plain Sight

Many locals will insist that **Mangel Halto** is the finest beach in South Aruba, and they make good points: the privacy of the sands, the little-used *palapas* (palm-covered shelters) and the fuzzy mangrove trees all around make for a glorious afternoon, before or after a trip to Spanish Lagoon next door.

The water is calm and the snorkeling easy, and there's no fee to visit. Note there are no lifeguards posted here.

Gold Mills

The crumbling stone walls of the **Balashi Gold Mills** recall nearly 100 years of gold mining in Aruba. Instead of a 'gold rush,' the nation saw consistent, industrial-scale extraction between 1824 and 1916, resulting in nearly 1.4 million kg of the precious metal.

Like the **Bushiribana Ruins** on the east coast, Balashi was ultimately closed and abandoned, but visitors to Spanish Lagoon can poke around these striking remains and imagine what life was like in the gold-harvesting heyday.

To learn more about this era, visit the **Museum of Industry** (p115) in downtown San Nicolas.

Above Mangel Halto beach

20 Sunset at SAVANETA

SEASHORE | SMALL TOWN | RELAXATION

Savaneta may be the most laid-back town in the whole country, which is really saying something. This seaside community of 12,000 is also known for being safe, friendly and dotted with boutique hotels. Outsiders are rarely aware that Savaneta is the oldest town in Aruba – and was once the island's capital. Come here to unwind, meet locals and take in soul-stirring sunsets.

HANS WAGEMAKER/SHUTTERSTOCK

How to

Getting around: Flat Savaneta is the perfect place for cycling. Otherwise, driving and walking are both effective ways to get around. For De Palm Island, board the ferry in the town of Balashi, right next to Spanish Lagoon.

When to go: This isn't a 'day trip' kind of town; to get the most out of Savaneta, stay a night or two and fall under its tranquilizing spell.

Ocean views: The best stays and dining in Savaneta are located right on the waterfront.

GLOBE GUIDE MEDIA INC/SHUTTERSTOCK

Far left top Savaneta
Far left bottom De Palm Island

Private beach Whether you call it Santo Largo or **Savaneta Beach**, this paper-white carpet of sand is as peaceful as it gets, and in the middle of a weekday, you might be the only one there. The beach is roughly divided into three sections, which are framed by stands of trees that lean lazily toward the lucid blue sea. Shallow waters make for effortless swimming and snorkeling, but note that the beach has no lifeguards at any time of day.

Night mission True to its name, **Clear Kayak Aruba** (clearkayakaruba.com) rents out clear-bottomed craft to outdoors people who want to gaze into the depths while they paddle. The company leads tours into nearby mangroves, and these two-hour expeditions make for arm-flexing fun during the daylight hours. Once the sun sets, Clear Kayak also ventures out at night, illuminating a path with LED lights and narrating the journey in English, Dutch or Spanish. Night tour participants must be at least 13 years old and not weigh more than 90kg.

Fresh catch **Zeerover** (facebook.com/zeerovers) is your classic down-home seafood restaurant, situated right on a weathered Savaneta pier. Boats of all types tie up right next to Zeerover (Dutch for 'pirate'), and picnic tables are set out on the wood planks. Grab whole fish on a plate or a basket of fried shrimp, then watch the sun melt into the horizon.

De Palm Island

Private *cabaña*? Check! Up-close interactions with flamingos? Check! Waterpark with twisting tubes that are lit up inside? You got it! **De Palm** (depalmisland.com) is a skinny barrier island off the southwest coast of Aruba, and for US$139 (US$115 for children aged nine and under), you can ride the ferry to this exclusive little theme park and spend the full day frolicking in the water or hanging out at the open bar.

Open from 10am to 5pm, De Palm attracts a curious mix of families and day-drinkers; extras include swims with a SNUBA (a kind of deep-water snorkel) and the inimitable Sea Trek (p121).

Scan this QR code for more information on the island.

21 Bond with NATURE

DONKEYS | LOOKOUT | UNDERSEA

Aruba is well endowed with natural wonders, and the best-known rocks and reefs lie in the north. Yet the southern side has its own majesty, which can be just as impressive and attracts smaller crowds. While they may seem further away from the big hotels and beaches, the Donkey Sanctuary and Mt Jamanota are each only 10 minutes from the airport.

QBICLE PHOTOS/SHUTTERSTOCK

How to

Getting around: You can hail a cab in downtown Oranjestad and arrive at either the Donkey Sanctuary or Mt Jamanota in 20 to 25 minutes.

When to go: Daytime hours are best for all activities. Mt Jamanota is open to the public from 8am to 4pm.

Bring water: These locations are all isolated, and you'll be glad you brought a reserve of water to hydrate with.

LUDO44/SHUTTERSTOCK

Far left top Mt Jamanota
Far left bottom Aruba Donkey Sanctuary

Nuzzle a donkey European settlers first brought donkeys to Aruba around 1500, and here they remained, grazing and laboring, for nearly five centuries. Tragedy struck in the 1970s, when a lethal disease spread through their herds and wiped out all but 20. The **Donkey Sanctuary** (main.arubandonkey.org/portal) was established in 1997 to protect the surviving animals; the population has since ballooned to 130, each with its own name and personality. You can visit these four-legged friends, and let them nuzzle you, any day of the week from 9am to 4pm; anyone (without severe allergies) is welcome to visit, and admission is free. The property looks like a very dry farm, with a visitors center covered in donkey murals. Falling in love? Fans can sponsor a donkey, and long-term visitors can sign up as volunteers in the sanctuary.

See above it all Flying into Aruba, you would think the tallest point on the island is Hooiberg, which rises prominently near Oranjestad. Yet the real first-place winner is **Mt Jamanota**, which stands just a little further south. Jamanota is also a scrub-encrusted rise, which strikes a much less dramatic profile than Hooiberg, but it's just a head taller, at 188m above sea level. There's a 3km loop trail that makes its way to the top of the mountain and back, or you can drive a car to the summit to take in its views of the rippling countryside. The final stages of the road are unpaved, but you should make it without a 4WD. Jamanota is free to visit, but note that dogs are not permitted up here.

Sea Trek

There are usually two major types of recreational dives: SCUBA and rebreather. But **Sea Trek** (depalmisland.com/signature-experiences/sea-trek) adds a third to the mix, the 'underwater helmet walk.' Like diving suits from the early 20th century, this futuristic headwear uses an oxygen line to help you breathe and roam around the sea floor, no tanks or flippers required.

The Sea Trek team has created a small playground, with a walkway and sunken Jeep, for explorers to interact with. The experience takes about 1hr and children as young as eight years old can sign up. To participate, you must already be a guest at De Palm Island (p119).

Scan this QR code for more information on Sea Trek.

22 Taste the Parrothead LIFESTYLE

DRINKS | MUSIC | SOCIALIZING

Patterned T-shirts and margaritas by the sea – that's how many envision Caribbean nights. The Beach Boys mention Aruba first in the lyrics to 'Kokomo', and Jimmy Buffett popularized the 'Parrothead' lifestyle through decades of songs, books and restaurants. If you're seeking out a row of easygoing bars and literal cheeseburgers in paradise, downtown San Nicolas is your spot.

How to

Getting around: Downtown San Nicolas, also known as the Zeppenfeldstraat area, is extremely walkable, with its wide sidewalks and handful of gridded streets. There aren't any hotels here, so plan to catch a taxi back to your accommodations.

When to go: Hit the nightlife early; most establishments in San Nicolas close around midnight.

Sex workers: Prostitution is legal and regulated in Aruba, and San Nicolas is its pretty visible epicenter.

Drinks Downtown

San Nicolas' nightlife district is wedged in between Helfrichstraat and Caya Captain R Rodger. The colorful old buildings in this area are sleepy during the day, but they liven up as the sun sets over the rooftops. One favorite haunt, just a couple of blocks from the central traffic circle, is **Chesterfield** (facebook.com/aruba.chesterfield); it's a festive little dive that attracts a wide range of customers and continues pouring drinks until 4am. Others along this row, like **Caribbean Bar** and **Carolina's Bar**, have a similar vibe: dark and casual, with a mix of tourists and (mostly) San Nicolas residents. Drinks are markedly cheaper here than in the north, and most conversations will unfold in Papiamento.

Tropical Eats

Two outstanding eateries are located within sight of the San Nicolas Visitor Center downtown: **Kulture Cafe**

IMAGE PROFESSIONALS GMBH/ALAMY

(facebook.com/kulturecafearuba) is a classy little option with coffee, wraps and paninis, as well as recurring jazz performances. Nearby is **O'Niel Caribbean Kitchen** (facebook.com/OnielCaribbeanKitchen297), a go-to for high-quality surf-and-turf; the menu also boasts a full page of house cocktails.

Other good spots in San Nicolas are scattered across town, and you'll have to put some effort into getting there. The standout is **Kamini's Kitchen** (facebook.com/KaminisKitchen), a peppy diner on the outskirts serving johnny cake breakfasts and curry-infused seafood for supper.

♫ Charlie's Bar

Charlie's Bar (charliesbararuba.com) is a legend in the Caribbean nightlife scene, both for its live music and robust personality. You can't miss it: a hand-painted sign covers the entire facade, and every wall is coated in traffic signs, license plates, vintage photos, dolls, buoys and lamps, among other memorabilia.

Established in 1941, Charlie's is one of the oldest businesses still operating in Aruba, and the history is palpable.

The menu includes seafood favorites and meaty mains, and regulars crowd around the small bar for beer and mixed drinks.

Scan this QR code for more information about Charlie's Bar.

Above Charlie's Bar

Birds of Aruba

AN UNLIKELY AVIARY

Aruba is for the birds – literally. Many travelers come just for the birding, thanks to the island's wealth of local species and importance to migrating flocks. Observant first-timers will spot more varieties than they expect, and seasoned naturalists will be keen to hit the trails with binoculars.

Left Flamingos
Center Pelican on a beach in Aruba
Right Black-and-orange troupial

PEYTON COLWELL/SHUTTERSTOCK

How many bird species would you guess there are in Aruba? If you added up all the winged creatures ever spotted – gliding over land, floating on water or perched on electrical wires – what would you estimate? Forty? Seventy? More? Try 280. According to Avibase, a global catalog, observers have confirmed sightings of 280 different avian species on the island, while more conservative databases still put this number well into the 200s. Many visitors are surprised to hear these astonishing figures; how does this dry patch of rock attract such impressive biodiversity, when fresh water is so scarce and trees cover less than 3% of the land? Yet despite this forbidding rock and cactus landscape, here the birds are, foraging and nesting on this unlikely speck in the south Caribbean.

Natives & Migrants

Naturally, many birds have lived on the island since time immemorial. You don't need to be an ornithologist to recognize ducks, pigeons and seagulls. You'll likely spot pelicans diving for fish in the many coves, as well as sandpipers scampering across the beach. But then there are less-known natives, like the black-and-orange troupial, or the tiny, yellow-breasted bananaquit, known in Papiamento as the *chibi chibi*. Birders will delight in these longtime residents, who have eked out a life in the brittle brush of Aruba's backcountry.

Meanwhile, scores of species spotted in Aruban skies don't live here full-time; instead they treat the island as a stepping stone on their migrations across the hemisphere. The island's close proximity to South America – just 24km from the coast of Venezuela – provides these birds with a

BLUEORANGE STUDIO/SHUTTERSTOCK

SABS.E/SHUTTERSTOCK

place to rest on their long journeys across continents, with most movement taking place during North America's autumn and spring. This is how so many beauties, like ospreys, yellow-billed cuckoos and rose-breasted grosbeaks, arrive in Aruba.

Newcomers

A few species came to Aruba with human chaperones. Take the flamingos: each day, a new wave of tourists arrives on **Renaissance Island**, where they admire the pink birds strutting through the wetlands. Many are unaware that flamingos don't come from Aruba, and they can't be found anywhere else on the island. While these long-legged waders are native to the Caribbean, these specimens probably came from nearby Venezuela or Bonaire. More dramatic imports are the ostriches and emus living at the Aruba Ostrich Farm (p95).

> Observers have confirmed sightings of 280 different avian species on the island. You'll likely spot pelicans, sandpipers, black-and-orange troupial and flamingos.

Their new home is a fitting environment. The island's climate nicely mimics semiarid regions like the Serengeti and Australian outback, making the island a comfortable place for these and other species to thrive. Look past the desert-like veneer and Aruba is a welcoming habitat; seabirds can feast on saltwater bounty, and burrowing owls can hunt for rodents in the grasses. Once you start looking, the landscape is suddenly full of songbirds, raptors and waterfowl. And you, too, might find yourself migrating here as the seasons change, searching the skies.

The Prikichi

The brown-throated parakeet is a cute little critter, the kind of yellow-green-feathered bird you'd find perched on a trapeze in a pet shop. Indeed, this species is related to other parakeets, and similar-looking relatives are scattered across the ABC islands, but its pale brown breast marks it as unique. Here it's known as the 'Prikichi,' and the species is so beloved in Aruba that it's known as the national bird.

They're abundant on the island; amateur birders can usually spot at least one on vacation. To increase your odds, look up at mango and tamarind trees; Prikichis love their sweet snacks.

Listings

BEST OF THE REST

Eat Up

Old Man and the Sea Restaurant $$$

Like Hemingway's novel, this restaurant centers on the water in a tropical location. Unlike the title character, you can enjoy New Zealand rack of lamb or glazed Thai sweet duck breast in a private gazebo accessible only by footbridge. Serving all three meals, Old Man may be Savaneta's finest restaurant.

Flying Fishbone $$$

This vast terrace is gorgeously lit up at night, and tables are often packed with Flying Fishbone regulars. Small wonder: the tuna tataki, lobster casserole and pasta portobello are delicious beyond words. Just save room for the decadent dessert menu. We recommend the chocolate ravioli.

Hangout Sports Bar $

Whatever your sport, team or favorite beer, the Hangout has got your back. Multinational flags hang from the ceiling, and global sports play on the TV. Regulars circulate around the pool table, and DJs spin in the evenings. Chomp classic pub food and follow up with a bottle of Presidente.

Battata Beach Bar $$

Rice, fish and a bottle of Balashi beer – what else could you ask for on a late afternoon in Savaneta? Battata is a no-frills, family-friendly joint with wicker chairs on the terrace and expansive views of the sea. The cocktails are multicolored and the burgers are the best bar none.

Marina Pirata Restaurant $$

There are no actual pirates at Marina Pirata, but it's located near actual marinas, as well as the mouth of Spanish Lagoon. Marina Pirata has specialized in seafood and classic Aruba cuisine for more than 40 years. Sit by the water and enjoy a range of lobster dishes.

Aruba Nautical Club $$

'Boat, fish and beer' is the motto of the Aruba Nautical Club. While the yacht club is a real institution, no membership is required to grab a table at the restaurant and dig into some fresh snapper. Great cocktails and gorgeous seaside views.

See & Do

Red Anchor

Beet-colored and standing nearly 5m tall, the Red Anchor is one of south Aruba's most recognized landmarks. It stands at a highway crossroads, and many passersby are surprised by the size of this 21,772kg monument. Recovered from the Caribbean's floor after an accident, the anchor honors mariners lost at sea.

MARTIN SZCZEPANIAK/SHUTTERSTOCK

Red Anchor

JADS Dive Center

JADS hits two dive sites a day, with a regular schedule that takes in the island's most popular destinations. While they offer boat dives and shore dives, the former are more highly recommended. Check it out at the western end of Baby Beach.

Aruba Bob Snorkel & Scuba

Aruba Bob provides each client with an underwater 'scooter,' which allows you to cover a lot more ground (nearly a mile of reef in a 90-minute tour) and makes it easier to dive down for an up-close look at the sea creatures. Tours enter the water from the beach at Mangel Halto.

First Aruba Masjid

A mosque, in Aruba? Inshallah, yes. This unexpected structure, with its yellow dome and twin minarets, stands on a rural patch just northeast of Spanish Lagoon, and serves as headquarters and sacred site for the Aruba Islamic Foundation. Most of the island's 1000 or so Muslims congregate here.

Palo Marga International Raceway

Start your engines! The Palo Marga Raceway hosts regular drag races in this dusty suburb north of San Nicolas, and thousands of locals turn out to cheer their favorite drivers. Catch global racers and motorcycle events as well.

ELINAXXIV/SHUTTERSTOCK

Seaglass and stones

Sea Glass Island

This thin barrier island was once used as a dump for Aruba's rubbish, but after years of oceanic forces, bits of glass have been softened into 'seaglass.' Today, Sea Glass Island is caked in these soapy, multicolored fragments. Paddle a kayak or hire a motorboat to take you to its gleaming shores.

Community Museum

Standing near the Museum of Industry, the Community Museum is more like a retrospective on local domestic life, with antique belongings and decorations spread throughout the old building. Formerly known as Nicolaas Store, the retail operation was lovingly renovated and opened to the public in 2017.

BONAIRE

UNDERWATER MARVELS | CULTURE | WATERSPORTS

RESEARCHED BY BAILEY FREEMAN

Practicalities

ARRIVING

Bonaire International Airport This tiny airport is the main point of entry, seeing connecting flights from Aruba, Curaçao and a handful of major cities like New York, Toronto and Amsterdam. It sits just beyond the south side of Kralendijk. Before you arrive, make sure to pay your tourism tax online – it's US$10 for residents of the Netherlands Antilles and US$75 for non-residents.

There are no boat connections unless you're on a cruise ship.

HOW MUCH FOR A

Bowl of iguana stew US$4

Windsurfing lesson US$50

Discovery dive US$70–100

WHEN TO GO

JAN–MAR
Bonaire's high season. Excellent weather, but more crowds.

APR–JUN
Pleasant shoulder season that's good for diving too.

JUL–SEP
Trade winds slow down and Bonaire is at its hottest.

OCT–DEC
Technically the rainy season, but showers pass through quickly.

GETTING AROUND

Car and taxi To really explore Bonaire, you'll need a car, as public transport is not common. However, if you're staying at a resort or working closely with a local dive shop, they'll often provide transportation or rent out their own vehicles. Bonaire also has a taxi system, but this won't be practical for traveling the island's more rural areas.

Walking Downtown Kralendijk is really the only walkable area, as the rest of Bonaire's restaurants, hotels and businesses sit more or less single-file along the roads ringing the island.

TOP: TIMOLINA/SHUTTERSTOCK
BOTTOM: GEORG BERG/ALAMY,
M UNAL OZMEN/SHUTTERSTOCK

EATING & DRINKING

Bonaire cuisine is similar to the food found on other ABC islands – proteins like chicken (pictured top right), barbecue and fish feature alongside salad/rice combos. Signature dishes include items like goat and fish stews, *funchi* (cornmeal fritter; pictured bottom right), *pastechi* (a fried savory pastry) and *tutu* (cornmeal and black-eyed peas). If you want to mix things up, Bonaire also has a surprising number of international restaurants for a small island, offering everything from Venezuelan to Italian to Dutch cuisine.

Best fresh fish Daily Catch Fisherman's Market (p145)

Must-try pastechis Pastechi House (p145)

CONNECT & FIND YOUR WAY

Wi-fi Access is standard – your best bets are hotels and restaurants – but don't expect much in rural areas. Cell signal is pretty good, but download directions just in case.

Navigation Most travel is via the island ring road. Some roads in the north can be rough, but high-clearance vehicles are really only needed in Washington-Slagbaai National Park.

WHERE TO STAY

Odds are you'll be staying in Kralendijk, the island's main hub for, well, everything. Outside the city, accommodation options are extremely limited; there are no places to stay in North End and the only place to stay in South End is Lac Bay.

Town/village	Pros/Cons
Kralendijk	Where the vast majority of accommodations are located; well-connected to restaurants and shopping
Sorobon	Home to a single breezy resort on the water; a bit limited food-wise

GAS

Gas is only available in Kralendijk, and it's a pay-before-you-pump situation. It's not the cheapest, either.

MONEY

Unlike its neighbors, Bonaire uses US currency only; ATMs are easy to find and most places accept cards. Skip the airport and head to local banks to exchange currency for the best rates.

KRALENDIJK & SOUTH END

TOWN VIBES | WATERSPORTS | HISTORY

RESEARCHED BY BAILEY FREEMAN

KRALENDIJK & SOUTH END
Trip Builder

Take in Kralendijk, Bonaire's laid-back capital city, and the unique beaches and dive sites on the island's southern half. Then spend a day exploring the area around Lac Bay – paddle the mangroves on the bay's northern rim or learn to windsurf at Sorobon.

Learn about Bonaire culture past and present at the **Terramar Museum** (p137)
4 minute walk from Fort Oranje

Snorkel the sloped reef at **Klein Bonaire** (p138)
35 minutes from downtown Kralendijk

Watch the sun go down at **Te Amo Beach** (p141)
10 minutes from downtown Kralendijk

Tour the largest mangrove forest in the ABCs with the **Mangrove Center** (p142)
20 minutes from downtown Kralendijk

Windsurf across the waters near **Sorobon Beach** (p142)
20 minutes from downtown Kralendijk

0 2 km
0 1 mile

Santa Barbara Crowns
Santa Barbara
Hato
Kaya Gobernador N Debrot
Antriol
Kaya Antonia
Kralendijk
Nikiboko
Kaya Nikiboko Zuid
Kaminda Sorobon
Kaminda Lac
Lac Bay
Belnem
Kaya Ir Randolph Statius van Eps
Bonaire National Marine Park
Caribbean Sea
Condenser Basins
Salt Pans

Practicalities

MONEY

ATMs are easy to find in Kralendijk, but not in South End. Have cash on hand for smaller establishments like food trucks.

ARRIVING

Bonaire International Airport is a five-minute drive from the city center. To get to South End, turn left on EEG Blvd or turn right to access Kaminda Sorobon and Lac Bay.

CONNECT

Wi-fi access is standard in Kralendijk and Sorobon, but don't expect much in South End. Cell signal is decent.

WHERE TO STAY

District	Pros/Cons
Halo	North of town, where many prominent dive hotels and resorts are. Atmospheric. Not very walkable.
Playa	Playa, aka downtown Kralendijk, has lodgings with the most urban feel. Not much nature.
Sabal Palm	South of town, higher-end and boutique hotels. Further from food options.

GETTING AROUND

Car You won't need a car in Kralendijk proper, though parking is easy. Rideshares are not available and taxi service is patchy. No transit services run to South End, so to visit you'll need wheels. Gas stations are only found in Kralendijk proper.

Walking Downtown Kralendijk is very walkable, but South End is not.

TOP: DARRYL BROOKS/SHUTTERSTOCK
BOTTOM: CACTUSBLUE.US

EATING & DRINKING

Kralendijk's food scene skews international, often with *krioyo* fusion elements. In addition to Dutch-inflected fare, you'll find Surinamese and Venezuelan, thanks to the island's proximity to South America. Most restaurants sit along the seafront and downtown; you won't find much in South End outside of Lac Bay and Te Amo Beach.

Best barbecue Bobbejan's (p137)

Must-try lionfish burger Cactus Blue (p145; pictured bottom left)

ALL YEAR
Kralendijk and South End are year-round destinations weather-wise, and the city hosts some fun annual events.

FEB
Carnival takes to the streets, though it's tamer than on neighboring islands.

OCT
Bonaire's International Regatta turns Kralendijk into a big party.

23 Stroll Kralendijk's DOWNTOWN

HISTORY | BOARDWALK | SHOPPING

Kralendijk may have a genial small-town feel, but all Bonaire roads begin and end here. Make its acquaintance by strolling its charming seafront, stopping at history museums (including the historic Fort Oranje) and browsing local shops.

GEMMA FLETCHER/SHUTTERSTOCK

What's in a Name?

Kralendijk is actually a city of two names. The Dutch Koralendijk – of which Kralendijk is a derivative – means 'coral dike,' referring to the coralstone on which the city was built. In the Papiamentu language, the town is called Playa, meaning 'beach,' and this is the name you'll most likely hear on the ground.

Trip Notes

Getting around: Kralendijk is the smallest of the ABC capital cities, and it's easily walkable.

When to go: There's no bad time to walk around Kralendijk, but things do get hot midday, and there's not a lot of shade.

Top tip: Looking to skip cruise-ship crowds? Check the schedules to see when the ships dock and unleash their passengers upon tiny Playa. Local blog InfoBonaire.com keeps a current list.

05 Keep heading north to end up at local favorite **Bobbejan's** – snag some of its famous ribs or chicken skewers to take away to your sunset-watching spot.

03 A block from the fort, you'll find the **Terramar Museum**, a small cultural space hosting rotating exhibitions featuring everything from historic coin collections and film screenings to work from local artists.

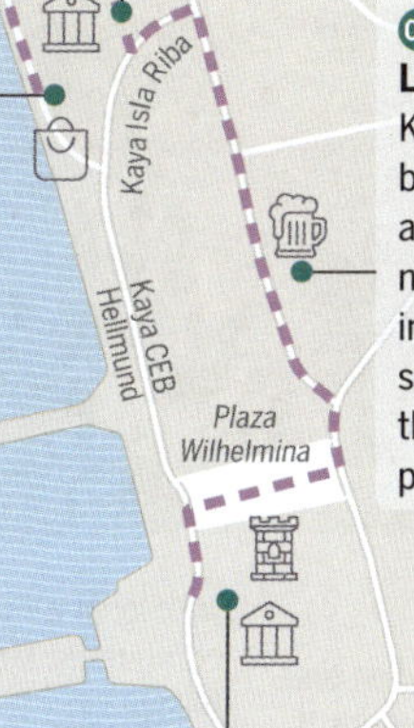

04 Adjacent to the museum you'll find a small studio called **MoltenWolf Glass**, which showcases glass art and jewelry made in house, as well as works from local artists of other mediums.

02 Wet your whistle at **La Cantina**, downtown Kralendijk's favorite brewery. It serves up a blonde ale that goes nicely alongside international eats. Be sure to snag a seat on the gorgeous central patio.

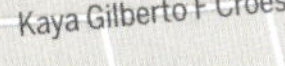

01 The first thing built following the Dutch acquisition of Bonaire was **Fort Oranje**. Restored in the late 1990s, the fort still greets cruise passengers and sometimes operates as a small open-air museum.

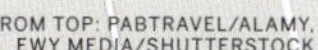

FROM TOP: PABTRAVEL/ALAMY, EWY MEDIA/SHUTTERSTOCK

24 Cruise to NO NAME BEACH

RELAXATION | BEACHES | SNORKELING

Klein Bonaire is a blip of a landmass right across the water from Kralendijk's seafront that makes for a pleasant afternoon trip for those who are self-sufficient – hop on the water taxi to lounge on the sugary sands of No Name Beach or take to the water to experience Bonaire's maritime treasures up close.

BYDRONEVIDEOS/SHUTTERSTOCK

How to

When to go: You'll be tied to water taxi schedules if you don't have a boat – we suggest avoiding the heat of midday.

Getting there: Klein Bonaire is only accessible by boat, and most book with local water-taxi companies. More on that below.

Tip: Klein Bonaire doesn't have any services on the island, so you'll need to bring everything – food, drinks, chairs etc – with you.

TUNATURA/SHUTTERSTOCK

CORA TESHEIRA/GETTY IMAGES

Klein Bonaire has had a varied past: first as a quarantine zone for arriving ships, then a grazing pasture, a charcoal production center and eventually a planned development site in the 1970s. However, strong local resistance led the Bonaire government to purchase the island and place it under the care of its marine park. Since then life has returned to the island en masse, and it's now an appealing combination of dry tropical forest, *salinas* (salt marshes) and beaches.

One of Klein Bonaire's major draws is **No Name Beach**. One of the few sandy swaths in the country, it's a doozy – long, pearly and backed by greenery. It makes for a lovely place to enjoy the afternoon.

If you're intrigued by what lies below the surface, grab your snorkeling gear and swim out to the drop-off (which is clearly visible from above the water). Here you'll find an explosion of coral and fish, and likely a sea turtle or two, as the island is a nesting ground for several species.

For a base price of US$25 you can take a water taxi out to the island (a 30-minute ride) and come back whenever you'd like, with the latest returns running at 4:30pm. **Epic** (watertaxi kleinbonaire.com) and **Caribe** (caribewatersportbonaire.com) are two of the main operators; the former also offers an upgrade that includes a beach chair and boxed lunch.

Far left top Klein Bonaire
Far left bottom Scuba diving, Bonaire
Left No Name Beach

Why I love Klein Bonaire

Klein Bonaire is what's called a Ramsar site, meaning it's protected, and you're not able to access everywhere in the light blue water. It's also one of Bonaire's most beautiful snorkeling spots, in my opinion.

It has a really steep, long cliff of coral, and the corals are a little bit bigger than around the rest of the island – the last time I went snorkeling I saw a hawksbill turtle and two really big lobsters! I think it's one of the most beautiful places we have here, because it is also protected – we're doing our job to inform everybody, to keep the island clean, to help everybody get in and out of the water.

By Myles Hayden, *head captain at Caribe Water Taxi*
@caribewatertaxi

25 Loop Through SOUTH END

SNORKELING | HISTORY | BEACHES

Driving through Bonaire's South End gives you a close look at the industrial history that has defined the island for centuries: the ring road encircles salt pans, while the southwestern side features some sobering historical monuments. Watersports enthusiasts will also enjoy this route: numerous dive spots are sprinkled along the way, as well as popular windsurfing sites.

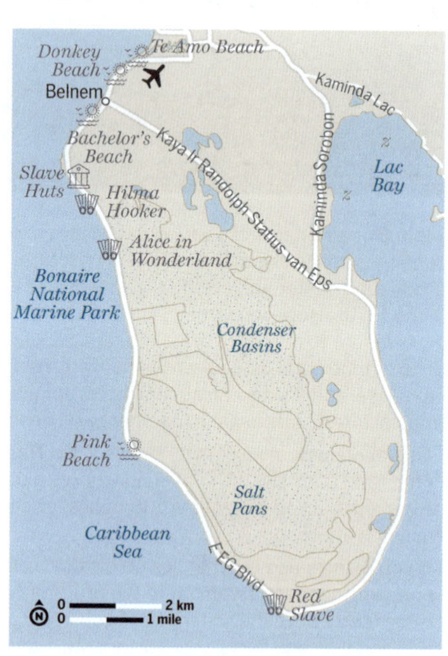

How to

Getting there: You're only getting here one way, and that's by car. The ring road is in good condition and well marked, so it's an easy drive.

When to go: Snorkeling is the main activity around these parts, so hit the water when the fish are most active: sunrise and sunset.

Tip: Grab dinner at Te Amo Beach from the **Stoked** food truck – the burgers are divine.

Most of Bonaire's southeastern side is inaccessible coastline, but you'll see several sculptures made of natural elements and plastic along the way – commentary on the Caribbean's battle against the waterborne trash that washes up on its shores.

On the western side of Bonaire closer to Kralendijk, you'll find more stops both above and below the waves. This is also where sobering testaments to Bonaire's history still stand. Stop at the **Red Slave** dive site and the **Slave Huts** further north to see the tiny domiciles that enslaved workers were forced to share as they worked the island's salt pans; its a visceral reminder of the cruelty that built Bonaire.

Along the rest of the coast you'll find more yellow stones marking official dive locations. For snorkeling, try out **Pink Beach** and **Alice in**

AQUAPIX/SHUTTERSTOCK

Wonderland; if you have dive gear, the **Hilma Hooker** spot marks a coral-covered shipwreck about 18m below. Some of these sites also double as lovely above-ground beaches. The aforementioned Pink Beach, **Bachelor's Beach** and **Donkey Beach** all make for nice options to post up and enjoy the sea breeze. When the sun starts to sink, make your way to **Te Amo Beach** for a stunning sunset and a convivial atmosphere – speakers bump everything from reggaeton to house to Afrobeat, and the vibe is nigh unbeatable.

The Strange Story of the Hilma Hooker

The *Hilma Hooker* has a bit of a cheeky story behind it. The boat was constructed in 1951 and functioned as a Dutch freighter until 1984, when customs discovered a whopping 25,000 pounds of marijuana aboard behind a false bulkhead.

It sat in the water off Bonaire while in legal limbo until the boat's pumps failed and the aged and only partially seaworthy *Hilma Hooker* began taking on water, eventually sinking.

Today it lies on its side 72ft below the surface and is home to spiny lobster, tarpon, barracuda and an array of sea sponges.

Above *Hilma Hooker* wreck

26 Treasures of LAC BAY

SNORKELING | WINDSURFING | WILDLIFE-WATCHING

Both nature lovers and adrenaline-seeking watersport fans will adore this little bay on the east side of Bonaire. Ringed with untouched mangroves – the largest in the ABCs – and flamingo-laden *salinas*, the bay is an eco hot spot, particularly for birdlife. Near Sorobon Beach, folks whizz across the water on windsurfing boards while music bumps from the amiable beach bars.

How to

Getting here: Cut east from Kralendijk on Kaminda Sorobon. Turn onto Kaminda Lac to head to the mangroves and Lac Cai. To get to Sorobon, stay the course as the road turns south and turn left when it dead-ends into Kaya IR Randolph Statius van Eps.

When to go: If you want to hit both sides of the bay, head out early.

Tip: Drive slowly on narrow Kaminda Lac and keep your eyes peeled for flamingos.

While most stick to the western coast for water activities, **Lac Bay** on the eastern side is a worthwhile jaunt for those who want to get active on the water beyond the dive scene. Here you'll find a beautiful blue bowl of ocean and estuary full of seagrass beds, a fringe reef and the largest mangrove forest of the ABC islands. It's also the preferred hangout of the Bonairian windsurfing community, with newbies and veterans alike whizzing across the water all day long.

Hang left on Kaminda Lac to observe flamingos in their *salinas* and connect with the excellent **Mangrove Center** for its sustainability-oriented kayak/snorkel tours. Take the night excursion to see another side of Bonaire's natural world – bioluminescence, anyone?

From there, continue down the road to affable **Lac Cai Beach**, a serene family-friendly spot with white sand,

HEDLEY LAMARR/SHUTTERSTOCK

shallow water and a peppy (if somewhat limited) beach bar. Look for the giant pile of conch shells, a remnant of pre-eco-protection fishing.

Stay the course on Kaminda Sorobon to arrive at its namesake **beach**, a bustling peninsula chock-a-block full of buzzing restaurants, convivial beach clubs and windsurfing outfitters – if you've ever wanted to learn how to ride a wave with an assist from the sea breeze, this is the place. Stand-up paddleboards and kayaks are also generally available.

Snorkeling Sorobon

The bright-blue bay is quite shallow, and it's possible to wade out to a small reef for some snorkeling via the Sorobon side.

Extreme care should be taken not to damage the corals, however, and you always need to keep an eye out for windsurfers; reserve this venture for extremely calm days, when it's easier to navigate the water and nobody will be trying to ride the wind.

Bonus: on the way out to the reef, you'll encounter expansive seagrass beds, home to sea turtles and the queen conch. Just remember to keep off the grass!

Above Windsurfing, Lac Bay

Listings

BEST OF THE REST

Souvenir Central

Jungle Concept Store

Colorful clothing store selling breezy-but-not-cheesy beachwear with tropical motifs; stylings have a modern resort-wear feel. Attached to the Art Hotel downtown.

Salt Shop Bonaire

Buy some of Bonaire's famous salt from this little nautical-themed shop on Kaya Grandi downtown. Culinary salt and bath products are both available, alongside local art and other tourist tchotchkes.

Something Special Bonaire

Homey souvenir shop with Dutch flair just down the way from the salt shop specializing in driftwood art of all kinds – ornaments, signage, sculptures and more – as well as jewelry and Dutch goods such as *stroopwafels* (waffle-like cookies).

South End Stops

Willemstoren Lighthouse

Located at Bonaire's southernmost tip, this lighthouse, built in 1837, was the first one constructed on the island. Nearby you'll find driftwood art sculptures built by local artists.

Donkey Sanctuary

Brought to the ABCs by the Spanish, wild(ish) donkeys are now a mainstay on Bonaire, and this sanctuary was established to protect them from human and animal harm. Drive the circuit to see the donkeys in their habitat, but be warned – they tend to block the path and are often in no hurry to move.

FX Kiteboarding School

Located just south of the Red Beryl dive site, this outfitter offers kiteboarding and, more unusually, windfoiling lessons. It also rents out bikes for use on Bonaire's trails. Private, beginner and semi-private lessons are all available.

Casual Kralendijk Eats

Between 2 Buns $

A sunny, relaxed, all-day place on the north side of town serving delicious mile-high sandwiches, salads and desserts – passion-fruit cheesecake, anyone? A local favorite for breakfast and lunch.

Maya's Corner Cafe $

Easily to find thanks to its bright-blue facade and giant flamingo mural adjacent to one of the main downtown parking areas, Maya's serves up coffee, smoothies, ciabatta sandwiches and rotating soups and stews. Don't miss the *bonchi*, a hearty dish with beef, oxtail, pumpkin and a smattering of spices.

UMOMOS/SHUTTERSTOCK

Salt pyramids, Bonaire

KRALENDIJK & SOUTH END REVIEWS

Pastechi House $

Grab an empanada-like pastry filled with whatever your heart desires – gouda cheese, smoked salmon, conch and more – along with *bitterballen* (fried meatballs), Johnny Cakes and smoothies.

Cactus Blue $

This amiable food truck at Donkey Beach serves hamburgers and wraps, and it's the only lunch spot serving up lionfish (a pro-environment choice, as lionfish are invasive).

Roos Surinam Food $$

Find a seat in the open-air atrium and dig into Surinamese classics like yellow chicken in coconut milk, chicken satay, beef rendang and roti of every variation. The ambience is casual and food is available for takeaway.

Rosa Cafe $$

Settle down in rose-pink surrounds to enjoy Italian pastries, sandwiches and other well-presented lunch/brunch fare. Don't miss the towering iced pistachio latte or the daily croissant combos.

Daily Catch Fisherman's Market $$$

A great option for self-caterers who want a taste of Bonaire's fresh seafood, this shop sells it by the kilo: grab some wahoo, barracuda or red snapper. The market also has a breakfast and lunch takeout menu featuring items like fish soup, fried fish balls and loaded fish tacos.

Food with a View

Karel's Beach Bar $$

This is a popular stop for cruise-ship passengers, so be prepared for crowds when the ships are in. It's also an inviting place to have a drink and a snack right on the water. Order a fruity cocktail and a conch fritter and enjoy the view out over the blue water.

ROSIE BELL/SHUTTERSTOCK

Willemstoren Lighthouse

Seaside Krioyo Fusion $$

A beach bar on the north side of town with a mid-century modern feel, this place serves slightly upmarket international dishes with *krioyo* flair. Come for breakfast if you want to avoid the late-afternoon crowds.

It Rains Fishes $$$

An upscale oceanside restaurant housed in a historic building along the main seafront, with a seafood-focused menu that embraces a variety of international preparations. It rains wine too – the list is lengthy.

Bars & Breweries

Sugar Thief $

Tex-Mex has made its way to Bonaire in the form of this friendly craft brewery – sip one of its creative concoctions and dive into some tacos in its sunny space on Kaya Inglaterra.

Hang Out Beachbar $$

Watch windsurfers cruise by on the bright-blue Lac Bay from the comfort of your beach lounger, cold Amstel Bright in hand. Head here for a classic no-frills-but-all-fun beach-bar experience.

NORTH END

CORAL REEF | NATIONAL PARKS | CULTURE HUB

RESEARCHED BY BAILEY FREEMAN

0 2 km
0 1 mile

Learn about Bonaire culture at **Mangazina di Rei** (p157)
20 minutes from downtown Kralendijk

Wander the trails of **Washington-Slagbaai National Park** (p154)
35 minutes from downtown Kralendijk

Salina Matijs

Salina Slagbaai

Washington-Slagbaai National Park

Rincon

Kaya Korona

Spy on flamingos at **Gotomeer** (p151)
35 minutes from downtown Kralendijk

Sample cactus liqueur at the **Cadushy Distillery** (p151)
23 minutes from downtown Kralendijk

Caribbean Sea

Santa Barbara Crowns

Peek at underwater marvels in the **Bonaire National Marine Park** (p158)
various points from Kralendijk

NORTH END
Trip Builder

Bonaire's North End feels alive – it encompasses stunning protected natural areas replete with wildlife and functions as a de facto cultural center for the island. Take your time and soak up all the ambience.

FROM LEFT: MINAS KEUKAZIAN/ALAMY, MICHELLE PETERS/SHUTTERSTOCK
PREVIOUS SPREAD: LINDA HORTON/SHUTTERSTOCK

Practicalities

ARRIVING

Bonaire International Airport Rincon, North End's main town, is a half-hour drive from the airport. You can access it from either side up the north loop road. The sometimes narrow north end road is an easy drive.

FIND YOUR WAY

Simply follow the ring road; the turn-off to Washington-Slagbaai National Park is in Rincon. Drive high-clearance vehicles in the park.

DRIVE WITH CARE

As you head north out of Kralendijk on your west-coast jaunt, N Debrot Blvd becomes the scenic Queen's Hwy – and a one-way route. The road is quite narrow and, unfortunately, you may encounter some folks driving the wrong way. Go very slowly and park with care.

MONEY

ATMs are plentiful in Kralendijk, but you won't find any in North End, so bring cash. Food costs less in these parts.

GETTING AROUND

Car and taxi You're going to need a car – ride-shares are not available and taxi services are patchy. No transit services run to North End. Be sure to fill up with gas before you leave Kralendijk.

Walking North End itself is not walkable. Downtown Rincon is walkable, but you'll still need a car to reach spots like Posada Para Mira and Mangazina di Rei.

TOP: HORIZONS WWP/ALAMY
BOTTOM: ROSITO/SHUTTERSTOCK

EATING & DRINKING

There's not much by way of food in North End outside of Rincon. The food here hones in on the local classics, saucy barbecue and *krioyo* dishes like goat stew (pictured top left), *funchi* (cornmeal fritters) and *tutu* (black bean and cornmeal side).

Best goat stew Cactus Fence Supreme (p164)
Must-try soursop ice cream (pictured bottom left) John's (p164)

ALL YEAR
North End is a year-round destination weather-wise, though things can get hot in September and October.

APR
Dia di Rincon features parades, concerts and plenty of food.

SEP
Several events aimed at encouraging beach clean-ups take place.

Get Cultured in NORTH END

MUSIC | WILDLIFE | CULTURE

Bonaire's North End is a tapestry of all the things that make the island more than just a dive hub – parrots flit between the trees, flamingos preen in the setting sun and Rincon hums with history. If you want to get to know Bonaire's culture, this is your stop.

PETER DOUGLAS CLARK/SHUTTERSTOCK

Trip Notes

Getting there: The most common route takes you northwest from Kralendijk on Kaya Gobernador N Debrot and onto the scenic Queen's Hwy. From here the road winds you through North End.

When to go: Anytime is a great time to visit this part of Bonaire. Come at the end of April to catch Rincon Day celebrations.

Tip: Business opening times here can be patchy because it's rural. Call ahead.

North End's Celebrities

Keep your eyes peeled for two of Bonaire's showiest avian residents: the brown-throated parakeet (aka the prikichi) and the yellow-shouldered Amazon parrot (aka the lora; pictured above). At first glance they look identical, but they can be identified by their beak colors – the parakeets have dark beaks while the parrots have light ones.

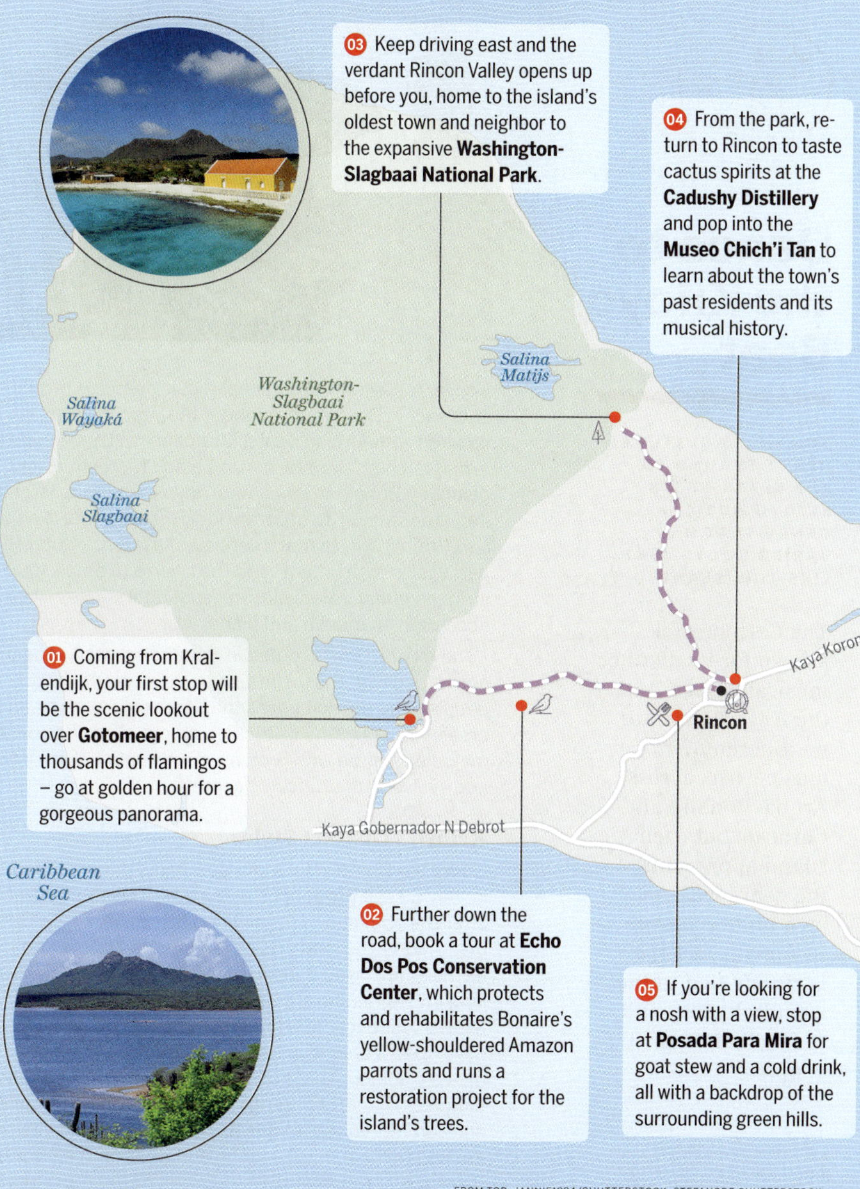

FROM TOP: JANNIE1994/SHUTTERSTOCK, STEFANGDE SHUTTERSTOCK

0 2 km
0 1 mile

Dance to the Krioyo Beat

BONAIRE'S CULTURAL HEART THRUMS TO THE BEATS OF ITS KRIOYO MUSIC, A GENRE THAT HAS VARIED ROOTS JUST LIKE THE ISLAND.

The Caribbean is known for its distinct musical genres, and the ABC islands are no different. *Krioyo* music exists across Aruba, Bonaire and Curaçao, but each island approaches the genre with its own unique flavor. In Bonaire, *krioyo* is closely tied to the island's history and the resilience of its people.

Left People playing the *wiri*, Rincon
Center Dia di Rincon celebrations
Right Museo Chich'i Tan sign

DPA PICTURE ALLIANCE ARCHIVE/ALAMY

Krioyo, the island's traditional music, features prominently at events in Bonaire throughout the year. It's a genre flavored with African beats, European waltzes and polkas, American jazz, Caribbean rumba and merengue, and distinctly Bonairian rhythms. *Krioyo* bands sing largely in Papiamentu and incorporate local instruments like the *barí* (drum), *wiri* (a metal version of a *güiro*, a Spanish percussion instrument) and the *kwarta* (a small, four-stringed guitar), alongside international staples like the accordion, mandolin and piano.

The music itself is rooted in Bonaire's history, one that's enmeshed with the institution of slavery – enslaved people used music to pass the time while working and to preserve links to their African cultures. Over the years, the melodies shifted with prolonged international influence and evolved into a specific genre.

Krioyo's Distinct Styles

Under the Dutch West India Company, Bonaire operated largely on salt production and animal husbandry, but after the abolition of slavery and the failure of the Dutch plantations, the land was sold off to merchants and formerly enslaved people, the latter often turning their land into agricultural *kunukus* (farms). The celebration of the harvest became known as Simadan, and eventually it developed a unique arm of *krioyo* music and a signature dance tradition. The music employs call and response, and features a handful of songs that always make an appearance on the set list. To this day, many *krioyo* festivities are tied to the harvest season and Simadan celebrations (February through April).

STEPHANKOGELMAN/SHUTTERSTOCK

NANCY C ROSS/GETTY IMAGES

Another type of Bonairian *krioyo* music is *barí*, which centers around the namesake drum and has its own unique rhythm and dances.

Where to Listen

The small town of Rincon is the epicenter of Bonaire's big musical tradition. While *krioyo* can be experienced on the island throughout the year, it reaches its fever pitch in April, with several festivals taking place throughout the month. Things kick off with the **Kanto Krioyo Festival** held at the Stadion Antonio Trenidat in Rincon, where the island's best musicians present their original work in a songwriting and singing competition.

> *Krioyo* is flavored with African beats, European waltzes and polkas, American jazz, Caribbean rumba and merengue, and distinctly Bonairian rhythms.

Later in the month, the party really heats up with the **Dia di Rincon** celebration, which is, you guessed it, a celebration of the town's history and culture – the party starts early in the morning and lasts all day, with folks arriving from all over the island to participate. The festival features Simadan parades and showcases featuring traditional and contemporary *krioyo* artists.

If you can't make it to Bonaire in April, you can also catch *krioyo* music at the **Nos Zjilea** cultural fair at **Mangazina di Rei**, which takes place at the end of each month. Otherwise, ask around – sometimes concerts pop up that aren't on calendars, but folks in the know can tell you where to go.

Get the Tutti Frutti

Want to get a taste of *krioyo* music before you hit the ground? Find the work of **Grupo Tutti Frutti** on YouTube – this band has been working for over 30 years to preserve traditional Bonaire music, and they make appearances at many events.

Learn more about *krioyo* music and Bonaire culture by checking out the **Foundation for Art and Culture of Bonaire** (bonaireartandculture.org), which runs several cultural preservation initiatives on the island, including the charming **Museo Chich'i Tan**.

Visits to the museum are by appointment, but are easy to arrange – just call the foundation.

28 Explore NATURE

NATURE | HISTORY | DRIVING ROUTES

Washington-Slagbaai National Park covers one-fifth of Bonaire. Formerly two plantations, these 5666 hectares were ceded to the government in 1969 and now stand as testament to the island's varied natural landscapes. Drive the park loops to take in mountains of coral stone, giant boulders delivered to the island's shore by an ancient tsunami and *salinas* home to local bird life.

GREENS AND BLUES/SHUTTERSTOCK

How to

Getting here: The park is easily accessible via Rincon.

When to go: Visit the national park early – there's not much shade and things get hot. All visitors must enter by 2:30pm.

Tip: If you've only got time for a brief visit, opt for the short loop (which takes roughly 90 minutes) or hike one of the two trails near the visitor center: Lagadishi or Kasikunda.

GREENS AND BLUES/SHUTTERSTOCK

Far left top Boka Kokolishi
Far left bottom Washington-Slagbaai National Park

Driving through history **Washington-Slagbaai National Park** encompasses dry tropical forest and craggy coastlines, and a visit here gives you the chance to dive deep into Bonaire's natural and human history.

The only way to explore the park is via two driving loops, a short and a long route. Indicated by yellow markers along the main road, the **long loop** takes 2½ hours if you drive straight through, but it will easily take up a whole day if you stop at the sights along the way.

Highlights include **Lagadishi Trail**, where you'll spy tons of giant cadushi cactuses, a dramatic coastal blowhole and views of **Playa Chikitu**. Next, head to **Boka Kokolishi** to relax in the tide pools hidden among the beach's boulders. Then continue to **Malmok** – here archaeologists have discovered evidence of humans dating back to 800 BCE. It was also a residential area for the plantation's enslaved people. Finally, birdwatchers shouldn't miss **Pos Mangel**, one of the two main watering holes in the park, and a natural home for several species.

Indicated by green markers, the **short loop** shares some stops with the long loop, but it omits the northernmost sights. Instead, it cuts straight west across the park and is the way to access **Brandaris**, Bonaire's highest point. The challenging hike to the top takes about 45 minutes, and the payoff is bird's-eye views of Washington-Slagbaai's forests, *salinas*, plains and coasts.

Park Pointers

Accessing Washington-Slagbaai generally requires a high-clearance vehicle, though park officials perform periodic maintenance on the roads after the rainy season ends, making them accessible to other cars. Ask a park official at the **visitor center**.

The park loops are one-way, so only begin the drive if you plan to see it through to the end. If you plan to hike Brandaris, the authorities require that anyone completing this hike enter the park by noon.

Washington-Slagbaai is also home to some exquisite dive sites, but they are currently closed for restoration.

29 Learn History on BONAIRE

HISTORY | CULTURAL EVENTS | MUSIC

Bonaire's existence as a colonial outpost is directly tied to the slave labor that built the salt industry here, and just outside of Rincon you'll find Cultural Park Mangazina di Rei, an important piece of this tragic history. Today, it also functions as a hub for celebrating Bonaire's traditional culture, hosting personalized tours and lively events.

JOKE VAN EEGHEM/SHUTTERSTOCK

How To

Getting here: The museum is a quick five-minute drive east from Rincon's downtown. It's also close to the island's cave drawings.

When to go: The Mangazina is open year-round, but only by appointment outside of Nos Zjilea; getting here takes some forward planning.

Tip: To fully understand the Mangazina's role on the island, be sure to visit the salt flats and **Slave Huts** on South End.

REMCO DE WIT/SHUTTERSTOCK

STEPHANKOGELMAN/SHUTTERSTOCK

Far left top Mangazina di Rei
Far left bottom White slave houses, Bonaire
Left Dia di Bonaire celebrations, Rincon

The Spanish were the first to harvest salt on Bonaire in the early 1500s, but upon acquiring the island, the Dutch turned it into a significant export. Enslaved people were forced to mine the salt flats on the southern end of the island in the hot sun without any form of eye or body protection; they would then make the 10-hour walk back to Rincon on Fridays to reunite with their families and get provisions from the storehouse that the cultural park now occupies.

Today, **Mangazina di Rei** (mangazinadirei.org) contains a small museum detailing Bonaire history and culture (and Rincon's place in it). Visits are by appointment and can be booked by emailing the park directly or contacting them via WhatsApp (info@mangazinadirei.org; +599 786 2101). The visits are guided, led by community elders who share their insight into island culture and Rincon, and they cost US$25 with an eight-person minimum.

The museum's most popular draw, however, is its **Nos Zjilea** event. Held on the last Saturday of every month, this celebration highlights different pieces of intangible cultural heritage, often featuring live music, food vendors and speakers who present on a variety of topics, including local crafts, medicinal practices, music traditions and more. For information on each month's theme, visit the museum's website.

Rincon's Importance

Rincon is the cultural cradle of the island. It has been inhabited for almost 500 years and is the oldest continuously inhabited village in the Netherlands Antilles; it was also the first capital of Bonaire. It was thanks to Rincon that the other villages came to exist – it was the first, and then when the enslaved people got their freedom, they departed to other villages like Tera Kora, which means 'red earth'.

Izaïn Mercera *is the experience coordinator at Mangazina di Rei*

30 Deep Diving in BONAIRE

SNORKELING | DIVING | CONSERVATION

An internationally renowned destination for underwater explorers, Bonaire National Marine Park is a shining example of how conservation and tourism can go hand in hand. Whether you snorkel or dive, this park astounds with its vibrant marine life.

JOHN A ANDERSON/SHUTTERSTOCK

How to

Getting here: The marine park is accessible via 87 public dive sites designated along the main road with large yellow stones.

When to go: Bonaire is a year-round diving destination.

Tip: If you plan on accessing the marine park (even for a quick snorkel), you need to pay the STINAPA nature fee (stinapabonaire.org; US$45) online. This is a separate fee from the tourism fee you pay upon arriving at the island.

ISABELLE KUEHN/SHUTTERSTOCK

History

Established in 1979 in a joint public-private effort between the Dutch government and the World Wildlife Fund, the **Bonaire National Marine Park** includes all the water off the island's coasts to a depth of 60m. Within this boundary divers and snorkelers will find over 2700 hectares of coral reef, mangroves and seagrass beds that are home to over 350 species of fish and 50 types of coral.

The park has strict no-anchoring laws for boats to protect the integrity of the reef, and while it's not technically as big as Belize's barrier reef, the coral cover is thicker and healthier, making it one of the best places to dive in the Caribbean – and the world.

LINDSEY LU/SHUTTERSTOCK

Stony Coral Tissue Loss Disease

While the reef is one of the healthiest in the world, it's not immune to threat. STINAPA is working to fight stony coral tissue loss disease, which is lethal to stony corals and spreading quickly across the Caribbean. Disinfect equipment between outings; the STINAPA website (stinapabonaire.org) has a map of the affected sites.

Far left top Coral reef, Bonaire
Far left bottom Eagle ray (p160)
Above Hawksbill turtle (p160)

Life Underwater

The variety of life that exists within these waters is truly breathtaking. Stony corals like the yellow great star coral, brain coral and maze coral abound, while fascinating creatures like dwarf seahorses, queen angelfish, green and hawksbill turtles, eagle rays and the occasional whale shark make appearances in the glimmering blue sea surrounding the island. The marine park protects some terrestrial animal species too, including the roseate tern, Caribbean flamingos and Bonaire anoles, as well as the island's mangroves near Lac Bay.

What to Do

Accessing the marine park is easier than you think, and that's part of Bonaire's draw – its unique fringe reef sits extremely close to the shoreline. For several of these sites, all you have to do is simply walk into the water, where much can be seen with just a snorkel.

Marine Park Rangers

STINAPA's boots on the ground are its marine park rangers – here a ranger shares information on some of the great conservation work they are doing.

'We have the King William Alexander Reserve and the Princess Maxima Reserve, where we really don't allow people to go in – not for fishing, not for snorkeling, not for swimming, not for anything – because the corals that you have down there on the reefs, we use them. If there's a species of coral that is not growing anymore on one dive site, we can take corals from the reserve and replant them on the dive site.'

Delany de Nobrega *is a ranger at Bonaire National Marine Park*

JOHN A ANDERSON/SHUTTERSTOCK

Far left Queen angelfish
Left Mangroves
Below Whale shark

For other sites, however, you'll need a proper dive set-up and sometimes a boat to see the wealth of life below the surface. That said, you won't need to take any crazy-long boat rides offshore. The marine park features 87 public dive sites, all labeled by large yellow stones along the road circumscribing the island. The vast majority of these dive sites are found along the western shore and encircling Klein Bonaire.

The STINAPA website has an excellent interactive dive site map – click each site for a short description offering info on access type, water conditions, expected fauna sightings and more.

FROM TOP: GAIL JOHNSON/SHUTTERSTOCK, BENEATH_ONE_BAR/SHUTTERSTOCK

Doing Your Part

Like all coral reefs, Bonaire's is an extremely fragile environment and much care should be taken to protect its biodiversity. When entering dive sites from the shore, use the established entrances into the water instead of forging new ones. As you peruse the reefs, avoid touching, kicking and standing on them, and resist the urge to follow marine life as they pass (particularly rays and turtles).

Get bonus points by using reef-safe sunscreen. If you're diving, it's mandatory to receive a Bonaire-specific orientation from your operator.

REEF LIFE
of the ABCs

01 Spotted eagle rays
These graceful beauties frequent the sandy floors of ABC shores, along with the rounder gray southern stingray.

02 Lettuce sea slug
This reef cleaner does indeed look like a couple of leaves of lettuce floating in the current thanks to its unique ability to photosynthesize the algae it consumes.

03 Green turtles
The largest of all hard-shelled turtles float through the waters of many Caribbean islands, including the ABCs. Head to the nearest sea-grass bed for the best chance to spot them.

04 Staghorn coral
These sharp-but-fragile corals are critically endangered due to ocean warming, but you can still spot 'thickets' of them in shallow waters.

05 Lavender stovepipe sponge
This extraterrestrial-looking creature grows in tall vertical cylinders, filter-feeding sea water as it flows by.

06 Sea fans
Sea fans are a type of soft coral that lives in

shallow waters with lots of waves, or down deep near strong currents.

07 Rainbow parrotfish
One of the reef's showiest residents, these beaked fish can grow over 1m long. You'll find them munching algae and other plant matter off shallow reefs.

08 Yellowhead jawfish
This quirky little creature burrows into the sand below reefs, hanging out in a hole until hunger strikes – then snatches any unsuspecting prey floating by.

09 Garden eels
One of the smaller eels in the Caribbean, these guys hide out in the sandy bottoms of reefs and eat plankton. Be sure to keep your eyes peeled – camouflage is kind of their thing.

10 Yellow pencil coral
A stony coral with protrusions that grow vertically and, you guessed it, look like thick yellow pencils.

01 MAYA_PARF/SHUTTERSTOCK, **02** JOHN A ANDERSON/SHUTTERSTOCK, **03** RICH CAREY/SHUTTERSTOCK, **04** JOHN A ANDERSON/SHUTTERSTOCK, **05** IMAGEBROKER.COM/ALAMY, **06** SEASHELL WORLD/SHUTTERSTOCK, **07** DINO STOCKS/SHUTTERSTOCK, **08** FOCUSED ADVENTURES/SHUTTERSTOCK, **09** SUBATOMICSCOPE/SHUTTERSTOCK, **10** ALEKSANDAR RUSEV/SHUTTERSTOCK

Listings

BEST OF THE REST

Classic Eats

Cactus Fence Supreme $

Drop in on this spot 1.5km north of Rincon for 'cold drinks and ambiance,' as the sign says, as well as some of the best Bonairian food on the island. Try goat soup, salted fish or another protein, all served with rice, *funchi* (cornmeal mash) and *tutu* (*funchi*, but with black-eyed peas and other seasonings). Only open on Sundays.

John's $

Pop over to this low-slung pink building in Rincon for scoops of homemade ice cream in a variety of fun flavors: in addition to the classics you'll find tamarind, soursop, rum raisin, avocado and more. A sweet way to beat the heat.

Kos Bon So $

Head to this local Rincon favorite for barbecue, fish, conch and occasionally live music. Things get busy around lunch, but the beer is always ice cold.

Foodie Experiences

Chefs Bonaire $$$

Located on the northern edge of Kralendijk on the Bamboo Bonaire property, this chef-to-table experience is a fun outing for hardcore foodies. The Dutch chefs bring out five impeccably plated courses that have optional wine pairings as well. Book well in advance.

Underwater Thrills

Karpata

One of the west coast's northernmost sites accessible from the main road, Karpata is a sprawling dive location that's a favorite of the marine park rangers. It offers plentiful elkhorn coral punctuated by old ship anchors, which give the place a bit of ambience.

Andrea I & II

These dive spots just north of Hato are great locations for beginner divers and snorkelers, with tons of soft coral and anemones. Keep your eyes peeled for seahorses and all three types of parrotfish, too.

1000 Steps

This place on the Queen's Hwy is worth a visit due to its abundance of star and stag coral; whale sharks also occasionally pass through too. The site is so named because the 64 steps down to the site entrance feel like 1000 on the way back up after a lengthy dive.

MARC A DUFOSSET/SHUTTERSTOCK

Karpata dive site

Cruz Seru Largu

Activities for Landlubbers

Bonaire Landsailing Adventures

Want to ride the wind without balancing on the water? Try landsailing with this business on Bonaire's east coast. Cruise the track in go-cart-esque vehicles powered by the sea breeze. Bookings are forecast-dependent, so stay up to date on the weather.

Wayaká Trail

A roughly 10.5km out-and-back hike through Bonaire's interior that shows off unique cactus, twisted wayaka trees, palu di sia korá trees (nicknamed 'tourist trees' because of their peeling red bark), land crabs, and plenty of bird life. The trailhead is off Terrace Rd, marked by a blue stone.

Tera Barra Native Garden

A farm-turned-conservation-project 8.5km from central Kralendijk that's dedicated to fostering the native plant species of Bonaire. Wander the grounds to learn about the island's flora or volunteer to help maintain the plants.

Local Landmarks

Cave Drawings

Five minutes east of Rincon down a short dirt road, these drawings echo Bonaire's pre-colonial past. The area is known as the 'star watcher's cave,' and it's believed that the Arawaks used the point to read the stars for date and time purposes; the drawings reflect these observations.

Cruz Seru Largu

Bonaire is largely flat, but Cruz Seru Largu offers a rare lookout point that delivers views of Kralendijk and the coastline from above. The cross adds to a nice sunset snap, too.

CURAÇAO

ART | HISTORY | FOOD

RESEARCHED BY BAILEY FREEMAN

Practicalities

SF PHOTO/SHUTTERSTOCK

ARRIVING

Hato International Airport Curaçao's airport sits on the northwestern fringes of Willemstad; it's about a 25-minute drive to downtown from there, so make arrangements to have wheels one way or another.

Cruise Ship Terminal Willemstad's other main point of access is the cruise port on the southern side of the city, which is within walking distance of Queen Emma Bridge.

Westpunt and the Southeast are primarily accessible by car from Willemstad.

HOW MUCH FOR A

Paddleboard rental US$20

E-bike tour US$85

Plate of red snapper US$20

WHEN TO GO

JAN–MAR
High season. Carnival is in full swing.

APR–JUN
Pleasant shoulder season with little rain. Peak turtle-nesting season.

JUL–SEP
Summer in the technical sense. Breezy and uncrowded.

OCT–DEC
Hot and damp, but rain passes through fast, often at night.

GETTING AROUND

Car and taxi To effectively explore the best of Curaçao, we suggest getting a car of your own, as beach hopping and exploring national parks are big parts of the trip. Taxis do exist but are quite expensive, especially if you're headed out of Willemstad. Some small-business drivers may make the trip up to Westpunt; you can ask at your accommodations.

Walking Curaçao's main walkable areas are downtown Willemstad, Mambo Beach and Jan Thiel. That said, you'll need a car to go between them, and everywhere else requires a car to get around. Westpunt and Sint Willibrordus are not generally walkable.

TOP: NINA FIRSOVA/SHUTTERSTOCK
BOTTOM: ISHY BOY/SHUTTERSTOCK

EATING & DRINKING

Curaçao's cuisine mirrors that of its neighbors, though this island seems to have a particular affinity for stews. Goat and chicken (pictured top right) stew are common, and you'll also see papaya stew, cucumber stew, plantain stew, cactus soup, okra soup, fish soup and more. Fusion food is also becoming quite popular on the island, marrying *krioyo* food traditions (pictured bottom right) with Asian, European and South American flavors. Eateries here range from casual to high-end-chef experiences.

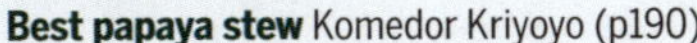

Best papaya stew Komedor Kriyoyo (p190)

Must-try modern Curaçaoan Kome (p181)

CONNECT & FIND YOUR WAY

Wi-fi The best internet access on the island is in Willemstad and its surrounds, with many (if not all) hotels and restaurants offering networks. Don't count on it in more rural spots.

Navigation Traffic may get hectic in Willemstad, but heading north and south out of town is easy. The roads are decent and well marked.

WHERE TO STAY

The majority of Curaçao's lodgings are in Willemstad, though a few resorts are located just north and south of town.

Town/City	Pros/Cons
Westpunt	A handful of smaller B&Bs and apartment rentals sit in fairly close proximity to beaches and national parks. Nearby food options are limited.
Willemstad	Accommodations of every kind, from boutique hotels to hostels. Atmospheric and walkable. Not close to any of Curaçao's bigger beaches.
Southeast of Willemstad	Luxury-oriented resorts with good tourist infrastructure, dive services and apartment options. A bit disconnected from the rest of Willemstad.

THE LANGUAGE OF HONKING

If you're driving around Curaçao, you're probably going to get honked at. This is usually more an acknowledgement than a correction.

MONEY

As of March 2025, Curaçao now uses the Caribbean Guilder (Cg). That said, US dollars are widely accepted, though you will get change in guilders. Euros are not as widely accepted.

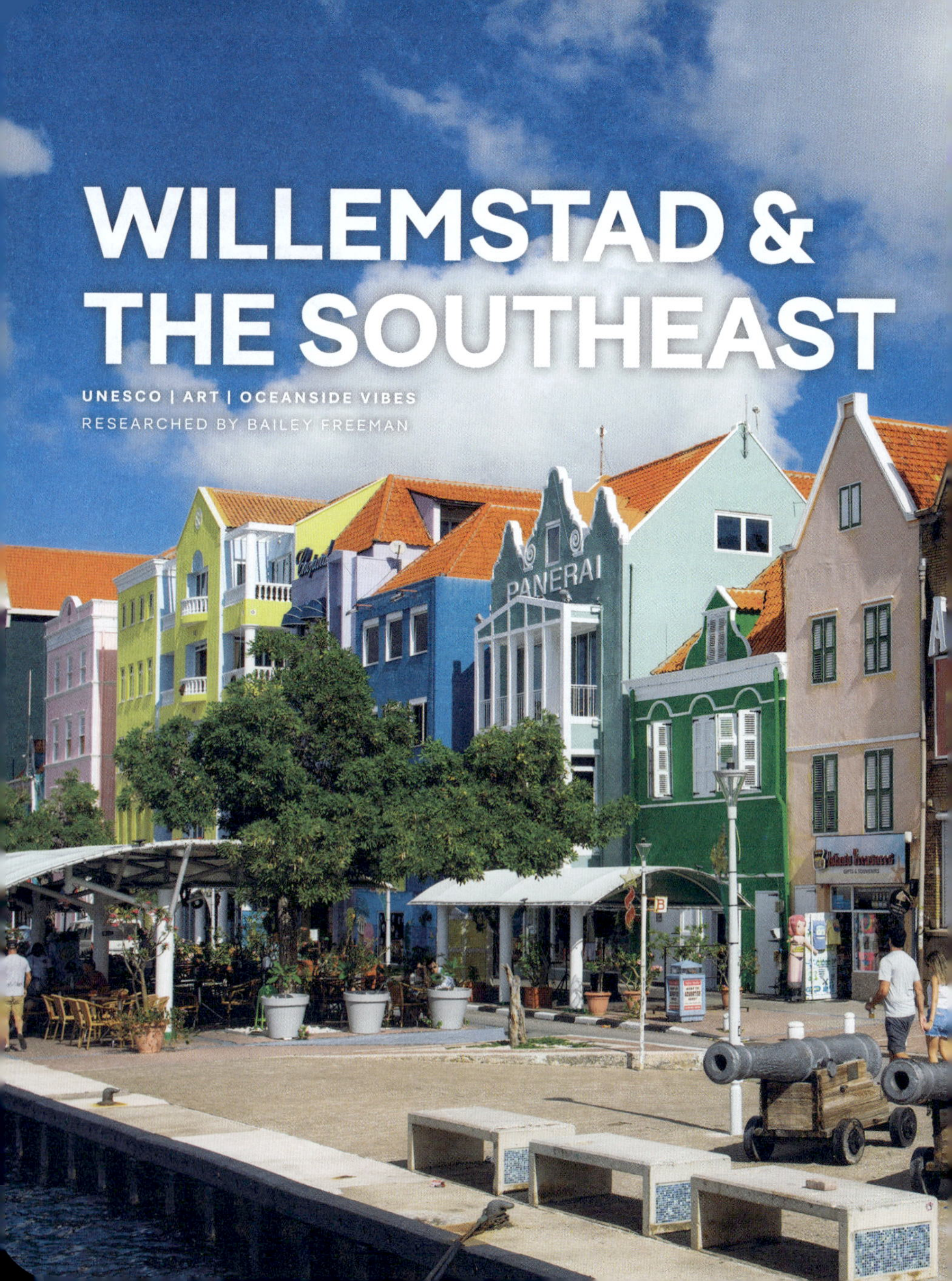

WILLEMSTAD & THE SOUTHEAST

UNESCO | ART | OCEANSIDE VIBES

RESEARCHED BY BAILEY FREEMAN

1708
PENHA
PENHA
FOR RENT
461-3049

0 5 km
0 2.5 miles

Weg Naar Santa Cruz

St Michiel

Piscadera Bay

Ring Rd

Schottegat

Willemstad

Santa Rosa Weg

Pietermaai Weg

Caribbean Sea

Spaanse Water

Tour **Otrobanda**, taking in the prolific street art found around every corner (p189)
2 minutes from Queen Emma Bridge

Learn about the island's signature liqueur at **Landhuis Chobolobo** (p175)
11 minutes from downtown Willemstad

Make your way to **Pietermaai** for an evening out with dinner and drinks (p181)
15 minutes from Queen Emma Bridge

Head to **Caracas-baai** for off-the-beaten-path beach hangs (p183)
22 minutes from downtown Willemstad

Head to **Mambo Beach** late for club vibes right on the sand (p187)
12 minutes from downtown Willemstad

Sip a cocktail at the manicured, relaxed beach clubs at **Jan Thiel** (p187)
25 minutes from downtown Willemstad

WILLEMSTAD & THE SOUTHEAST

Trip Builder

Buzzy Willemstad will be your port of entry to Curaçao, and it's arguably the liveliest capital town in the ABCs. Southeastern Curaçao offers good options for those looking for island activities with more amenities than you'll find in Westpunt.

ABOVE: JOKE VAN EEGHEM/SHUTTERSTOCK
PREVIOUS SPREAD: WANGKUN JIA/SHUTTERSTOCK

Practicalities

MONEY

Willemstad is replete with quick-pay options. ATMs abound and cards can be used most places. Same goes for the southeast.

ARRIVING

Hato International Airport, Curaçao's airport, sits on the northwestern fringes of Willemstadt. It's a 25-minute drive to downtown from there, so arrange a car.

CONNECT

The best internet access is in and around Willemstad; hotels, restaurants and museums generally have wi-fi networks available.

WHERE TO STAY

Area	Pros/Cons
Punda	In the heart of walkable Willemstad. Limited hotel options.
Otrobanda	Hostels and apartment rentals, but a few boutique hotels too.
Pietermaai	Cute boutique hotels line this neighborhood stretch. Artsy, relaxed vibe.
Jan Thiel	Resorts and large-scale apartment rentals. Great for families. Can feel sterile.

GETTING AROUND

Car and taxi You'll need wheels to reach Jan Thiel, Mambo Beach and Caracasbaai. There are no rideshare services on the island. Taxis are available and they charge government-regulated fares.

Walking Willemstad is a walkable city, even between neighborhoods, so slap on a pair of comfy shoes and make the city your oyster.

TOP: ZINA SELETSKAYA/SHUTTERSTOCK
BOTTOM: GEORG BERG/ALAMY

EATING & DRINKING

Cuisine ranges from traditional ABC island fare to experimental chef-driven joints. Around downtown, Pietermaai offers many hip choices as well as nice waterfront options. Further afield, Mambo Beach and Jan Thiel offer a variety of restaurants, while local favorites are dotted around the city's northern half.

Best classic Curaçaoan cuisine Plasa Bieu (p175; pictured bottom left)

Must-try fresh seafood De Visserij (p181)

ALL YEAR
Weather-wise, Willemstad and the southeast are year-round destinations; plan your time in the city based on cultural events.

FEB
Carnaval takes over in riotous color.

AUG
The Kaya Kaya Festival turns Otrobanda into an open-air concert.

31 Willemstad in ONE DAY

HISTORY | MUSIC | FOOD

Breezy Willemstad makes for a well-rounded wander – from history museums to foodie hangouts to natural oases, you'll be able to get a taste of this vibrant city on foot. If you have wheels, you'll be able to discover some bonus experiences, too.

FOTOS593/SHUTTERSTOCK

Trip Notes

Getting around: Willemstad is easy to navigate on foot; just wear a good pair of shoes.

When to go: Willemstad is great any time of year; if you're a party animal, hit the city during Carnaval in February or in August for Otrobanda's Kaya Kaya Festival or the North Sea Jazz Festival.

Tip: Willemstad isn't exactly a budget destination, but you'll find the lowest prices September through November.

Punda Vibes

In town on a Thursday? Punda comes alive from 6pm to 10pm for Punda Vibes, a neighborhood-wide party with live music and fireworks.

Most venues in the area will be hosting bands; catch the fireworks show from the uber-mod **Cascada Rooftop Bar**, cocktail in hand.

03 Nearby sits the **Maritime History Museum**, which covers Curaçao's seafaring legacy from maritime exploration in the Middle Ages to 20th-century cruise-ship tourism.

05 Pop over to **Landhuis Chobolobo** to learn about the making of one of the most famous liqueurs in the Caribbean: blue curaçao. Stick around at the bar afterwards for fun drinks.

Schottegat

04 Grab lunch at buzzy **Plasa Bieu**, the old food market and your best bet for finding classic Curaçaoan cuisine – portions are huge. Don't skip the red snapper! And be sure to bring cash.

Ring Rd

Queen Juliana Bridge

Breedestraat

Kijkduinstraat

President R Betancourt Blvd

Schottegatweg

OTROBANDA

Scharlooweg

Berg Altena

De Ruyterkade

Pietermaai

Penstraat

Caribbean Sea

01 Start in **Otrobanda** heading east to snap a photo on the iconic **Queen Emma Bridge**, a pontoon floating in front of colorful **Punda**.

02 Head to **Scharloo**, location of some of the city's first wharfs and later the homes of the island's Jewish merchants, to visit the **Jewish Cultural-Historical Museum**, the oldest synagogue in the Americas.

FROM LEFT: FOKKE BAARSSEN/SHUTTERSTOCK, DARRYL BROOKS/SHUTTERSTOCK

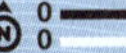

32 Explore Curaçao's HISTORY

HISTORY | CULTURE | ARTIFACTS

You'll will notice that almost every site you visit – museums, national parks, even beaches – sits on a former plantation. Learn more about the role the island played in slavery in the Caribbean in the 17th, 18th and 19th centuries at the Museum Kura Hulanda.

ULLSTEIN BILD/GETTY IMAGES

How to

Getting here: Museum Kura Hulanda sits in the heart of Otrobanda, and is within walking distance of downtown Willemstad's major attractions.

When to go: Kura Hulanda is open seven days a week year-round.

Tip: Allow yourself plenty of time to fully take in the vast amount of heavy information here; this is a museum that should be entered with reverence and attention.

SERGE YATUNIN/SHUTTERSTOCK

LINDA THOMPKINS/500PX

Far left top and bottom Museum Kura Hulanda
Left Entrance, Museum Kura Hulanda

Downtown Willemstad was deemed a UNESCO World Heritage Site in 1997, and it's home to nearly 800 official historical monuments strewn across the historic districts of Otrobanda, Punda, Scharloo and Pietermaai.

But rainbow-colored Willemstad was built over the course of centuries by something much darker: the terrible legacy of the Dutch West India Company and its pivotal role in the transatlantic trafficking of enslaved human beings. Curaçao was one of the main transfer ports for enslaved people in the Caribbean, and millions passed through its markets on the way to plantations in North and South America, and the rest of the region. The trafficking of enslaved Africans was the island's primary economic driver until its abolition in 1863.

The main exhibits at **Museum Kura Hulanda** in Otrobanda delve into the terrible role the institution played in Curaçao. On display are cultural artifacts from those who were trafficked, historical information about the Dutch West India Company and slavery in Curaçao, and heartbreaking and visceral artifacts from the system itself. The most impactful room features a to-scale recreation of a claustrophobic slave-ship galley and the restraints that would have been in place.

Other galleries examine slavery and racism in the US, while others delve into the African cultures that now make up part of Curaçao's heritage.

Kura Hulanda Village

Somewhat jarringly, the Kura Hulanda Museum is located within a colorful shopping and dining complex called **Kura Hulanda Village** that is encompassed by the UNESCO certified downtown area. Colorful murals, patio bars and art galleries abound should you need a place to escape the hot Caribbean sun and/or ponder the contents of the museum.

Pop into the gorgeous gallery of artist, muralist and designer **Bagira**, whose gorgeous mural covers a prominent wall in the village, or grab a fresh-from-the-sea *crudo*, small plates and a refreshing cocktail at **Caleo**.

33 Marvel at the ART SCENE

HISTORY | ART | CULTURAL EVENTS

Curaçao's juggernaut of an art scene includes all disciplines, and much attention has been given to fostering the creative community on the island. Landhuis Bloemhof is an essential stop for anyone interested in learning more about visual art in the ABCs.

GAIL JOHNSON/SHUTTERSTOCK

How to

Getting here: The museum is around a 15-minute drive from Punda, and there's on-site parking.

When to go: Bloemhof is open year-round.

Check the Facebook page (facebook.com/LandhuisBloemhof) for cultural events.

Tip: Check the events calendar for concerts, art classes, film screenings and craft fairs hosted on the grounds.

CATHEDRALOFTHORNS.COM

CATHEDRALOFTHORNS.COM

For a taste of contemporary Curaçao, make the quick drive over to **Landhuis Bloemhof**. Like many of the 'country houses,' on the island, Bloemhof was originally a water plantation, and enslaved people worked on the estate. Today it has been converted into a cultural center highlighting the talent of Curaçaoan and other Caribbean artists, exhibiting work in all mediums. The exhibitions largely rotate except for the preserved studio of May Henriquez, the sculptor and former resident whose artistic legacy inspired the creation of the museum.

Take in the exhibition in the main gallery, wander the trails behind the house for pop-up art installations, meet sculptor **Hortence Brouwn** in her outdoor studio or walk over to the museum's headline attraction, the impressive **Cathedral Labyrinth of Thorns**, made by artist Herman van Bergen. This giant maze/gallery is made entirely of bush thorns from the Acacia tortuosa, and it brings a fantastical element to the Bloemhof grounds.

Beyond the cathedral is a short walking trail that winds through native shrubbery to arrive at a pocket of trees decorated with books – a whimsical hidden treat for those who take the time to look for it.

If you're feeling a bit peckish, the museum also has a beautiful onsite cafe – **Number Ten** – that serves up coffee, sandwiches and gorgeous cakes; be sure to snag a seat on the leafy patio for maximum vibes.

Far left top Landhuis Bloemhof
Far left bottom and left Cathedral Labyrinth of Thorns

May Henriquez' Legacy

May Henriquez' grandmother purchased the house in 1919, and upon inheriting the property herself, Henriquez and her husband Max opened the estate as a salon of sorts in the 1940s, beginning its history as a meeting place for Caribbean artists and creatives.

Throughout her life, Henriquez worked as a sculptor, painter and writer, translating plays into Papiamentu and composing original stories based on Curaçao's culture and history.

She also published studies on the impact of Curaçao's Sephardic Jewish community (of which she was a member) on the development of Papiamentu as a language.

34 Taste Willemstad's CUISINE

LOCAL CUISINE | GORGEOUS DRINKS | INTERNATIONAL FUSION

Despite being an established hub for cruise ships and tourism in general, Willemstad offers a culinary scene that feels varied and authentic, with each neighborhood offering a number of great bars and restaurants no matter the time of day. Pace yourself and dive into Curaçao's ultimate foodie experience.

MULEVICH/SHUTTERSTOCK

How to

Getting around: Anywhere downtown is walkable; you'll need a car to go further afield.

When to go: The only time you'll struggle to find a place to nosh is that weird late-afternoon block between 2:30pm and 4:30pm when lunch spots are closed and dinner spots haven't opened yet.

Tip: Always check to see if a restaurant requires reservations – many fancier dining rooms are small and should be booked ahead.

JON ARNOLD IMAGES LTD/ALAMY

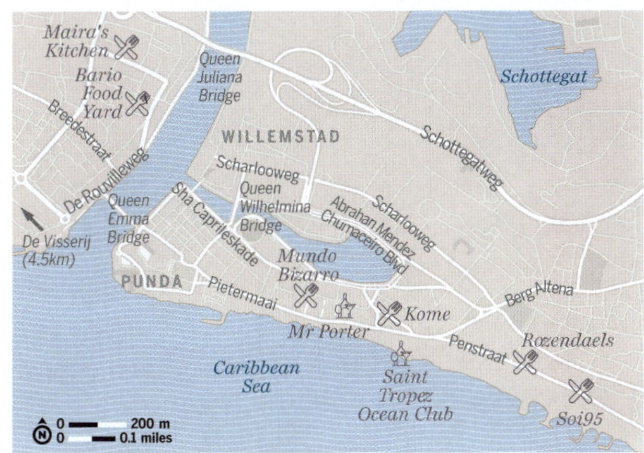

When it comes to eating and drinking, Otrobanda and Pietermaai are your best bets for truly fun fare. Both formerly neglected neighborhoods have become creative centers thanks to massive local efforts, and together they give Willemstad its zing.

In Otrobanda, head straight to sunny **Maira's Kitchen** for an impressive house breakfast and a lunch menu featuring both Curaçaoan and Dutch classics. For happy hour or dinner, don't miss **Bario Food Yard**, adjacent to the hotel of the same name; the food caters to all tastes and the drinks are good too. Further west, **De Visserij** remains a longtime favorite for fresh seafood, from shrimp to tuna.

Pietermaai is home to several of Willemstad's forward-thinking Caribbean tastemakers. Try elevated international fare with a Curaçao twist at **Kome** (which means 'eat' in Papiamentu), or venture further down Penstraat for Dutch-Caribbean dishes like *keshi yena* (pulled chicken with gouda cheese) and coconut fish at **Rozendaels**. The modern Asian creations at **Soi95** are also massive local hits.

The Pietermaai neighborhood is also where Willemstad's nightlife comes alive. Those looking for a place to see and be seen should head to the posh **Saint Tropez Ocean Club** and sip cocktails on the pool deck overlooking the sea. If you're ready to dance, head to the Cuba-inspired **Mundo Bizarro** for live music and a party that spills onto the street. Down the road, **Mr Porter** shares a jovial party atmosphere with a few other bars in its immediate vicinity.

Far left top Cafe, Willemstad
Far left bottom Saint Tropez Ocean Club

Krioyo Fusion in Willemstad

A lot of restaurants are opening now and there's a new vibe; they take the traditional food from Curaçao and fusion it. *Bario* means 'neighborhoods,' so we take [inspiration] from neighborhoods from all around the world – some influence from South America, Japan, some Dutch, South Indian, Caribbean – and we mix it together to create new dishes.

On Curaçao we import a lot of things, but now we've also started to grow our own products. A lot of restaurants have started to work with these farmers to sustain the local community.

Heinrich Hortencia *is head chef and co-owner of Bario Food Yard @chefheinrichhortencia*

35 Enjoy a Caribbean ADVENTURE

CORAL REEF | ISLANDS | SPORTS

Curaçao is fringed with beautiful, clear waters punctuated by colorful coral reefs, and a visit here would be incomplete without experiencing the plethora of water activities the island offers. Spend the day on a nearby uninhabited island, witness the reef's technicolor wildlife or paddleboard through mangroves.

NATUREPICSFILMS/SHUTTERSTOCK

How to

Getting here: Tour operators abound, and they'll likely be the ones coordinating your transport and gear rentals.

When to go: Curaçao doesn't experience hurricane season, so your odds are good throughout the year. That said, prices do go up in the travel high season of December through April.

Tip: The best (and most responsible) way to experience wildlife is to keep your distance, so if the tour operator you're considering promises close encounters or touch experiences, find another.

GREENS AND BLUES/SHUTTERSTOCK

Snorkeling

You don't have to be dive certified to get a glimpse of some of Curaçao's underwater treasures – the island is home to several great snorkeling spots accessible from shore. The best snorkeling spots in the southeast sit down in Caracasbaai: **Director's Bay** and **Tugboat** (an actual sunken boat covered in coral) are its biggest hits. In Westpunt, **Playa Porto Mari**, **Kleine Knip** and **Playa Lagún** also offer excellent snorkeling options straight from the beach.

JOKE VAN EEGHEM/SHUTTERSTOCK

Diving

If you do have a diving certification (or plan on completing one while you're in Curaçao), another world of underwater exploration

Get a Dive Certificate

Don't have your diving certification yet? Plenty of outfitters can set you up with dive-course materials, discovery dives and open-water dives. If diving is the whole point of your trip, you may want to kill two birds with one stone and book a dive resort, which can coordinate the whole thing for you.

Far left top Tugboat, Caracasbaai
Far left bottom Playa Lagún
Above Director's Bay

opens to you. Hop in a boat to access sites like the **Mushroom Forest**, the **Double Reef** and **Smokey's**.

Klein Curaçao

Klein Curaçao is a place shaped by its past – the island was scraped clean due to phosphate mining in the 19th century – but it's on the mend. Reforestation efforts have brought back the seabirds that have historically roosted here (including some rare species), and the waters teem with fish and sea turtles. A trip here reveals the regenerative power of nature.

Take a dip in its spectacular water, the clarity and color of which can't be overstated. Spot lots of small schooling fish beneath the waves, and lucky folks will also see some sea turtles – Klein Curaçao is a nesting ground for green and hawksbill turtles, and conservationists actively monitor the nesting activity here.

Klein Curaçao sits 10km from Curaçao and is only accessible by boat. No public water taxis

Diving for Beginners

Curaçao has warm water temperature, good visibility, no strong currents and easy entries. We do a lot of shore diving, so you can just walk into the water and dive straight away. You don't have to go out by boat.

Sometimes people – especially in the beginning, when they're learning – have problems with equalizing. But because we walk in from the shore, you can equalize slowly as you follow the reef down. You have all the time you need to adjust.

Daan Drechsel *is the owner of Dive Center Pietermaai @divecenterpietermaai*

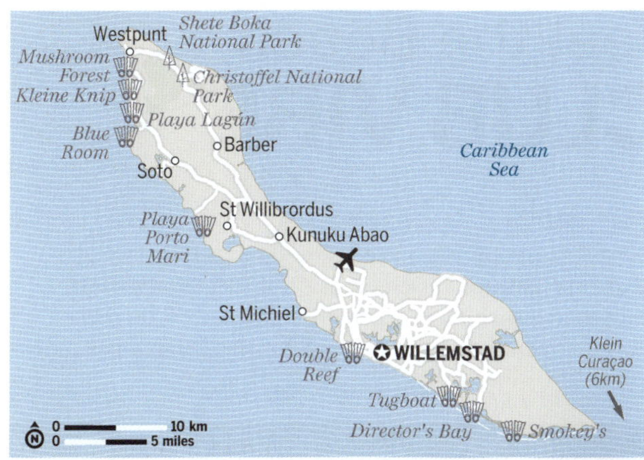

Left Blue Room
Below Mushroom Forest

make the trip, only private tour companies, the most well-known of which are **Mermaid** and **Miss Ann Boat Trips**, which depart from Caracasbaai.

Paddleboarding

If you'd rather stay above the water's surface, book a stand-up paddleboard session with **SUPCuraçao** on **Spaanse Water** (aka Spanish Water); here you can float along on the currents of the naturally occurring harbor and admire the beauty of the mangroves up close – keep your eyes peeled for egrets and herons! Architecture nerds will also enjoy views of the hillside villas encircling the harbor. Kayaking options are available here too.

Blue Room

Have you ever been to an underwater cave? **Blue Room** is a good spot for snorkelers and divers, and can be accessed by boat or by a trail leading from **Playa Santa Cruz**. Head over in the afternoon, when the sun sits overhead and lights up the bright blue water, seemingly from below. Here you'll spot plenty of schooling fish. Ease of accessibility does vary with the tides: if you come when the water is high, you'll have to swim underwater to access the room. If it's low, you can enter on the surface.

FROM LEFT: NATUREPICSFILMS/SHUTTERSTOCK, HUMBERTO RAMIREZ/GETTY IMAGES

36 Feel the Beach CLUB VIBE

LOUNGERS | COCKTAILS | RELAXATION

Curaçao's south coast exists in opposition to its large, nature-oriented north. Its main attractions are the curated beach clubs on Willemstad's south end, which offer a beach experience with all the amenities while still largely avoiding the pitfalls of high-rise coastal developments. Sit down, grab a cocktail (or mocktail!) and let the chill ABC vibes roll.

BYDRONEVIDEOS/SHUTTERSTOCK

How to

Getting here and around: You'll need a car to reach most of Curaçao's beach clubs. The areas in and around Mambo and Jan Thiel are walkable, but you can't walk between the two.

When to go: Beach clubs are all-day attractions; some turn into proper nightlife clubs when the sun goes down.

Tip: Double-check which clubs require lounger reservations versus which ones accept walk-ups. It's always best to reserve your spot ahead of time.

DAVID ENGLISH/SHUTTERSTOCK

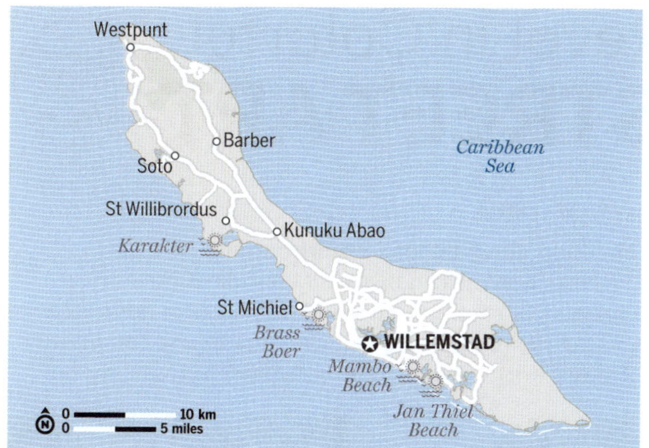

Heading south from Willemstad, **Mambo Beach** will be the first beach area you'll encounter. Here you'll find a small mall 'boulevard' full of shops and restaurants overlooking the beach itself. Access the sands via the area's beach clubs: **Bonita Beach Club**, **Madero Ocean Club**, **Riléks Beach Bar** and **Wet & Wild**. Loungers and *cabañas* are available for rent, and each club features its own restaurant/bar. Mambo is also one of Curaçao's best nightlife spots, with Madero and Wet & Wild converting into beach dance floors with DJs late into the night. **Hemingway** (part of **Lions Dive & Beach Resort**) is also a popular hang.

A quick 15-minute drive down the road will take you to **Jan Thiel Beach**. The set-up is similar to Mambo in that the beach is paid access, but this area feels less party-centric, swapping shops and foot traffic for a smattering of restaurants. Here, favorite beach club/restaurants include **Koko's** and **Zanzibar**. When it comes to late-night partying here, Zanzibar is the place to be.

North of town you'll find a couple of other more low-key clubs. The **Brass Boer** at the Blue Bay Curaçao Golf & Beach Resort offers a culinary-centric experience and rentable beach sunbeds, and **Karakter** at Coral Estate is nice if you're looking for sun and spa offerings, but not necessarily sand.

Far left top Mambo Beach
Far left bottom Jan Thiel Beach

Diving Near Jan Thiel

While Jan Thiel may be manicured and relaxation-oriented topside, it's also a jumping-off point for some good diving opportunities, with several shore and boat dive sites in the area: **Sweet Bottom** and **Sandy's Plateau** highlight the wildlife that live in the sandy shallows, while the **Diver's Leap** and **Beacon Point** show off coral in wall and pillar form. The **Jan Thiel Bay** site offers a nice mix of all of the above, plus a shipwreck.

Book with one of the outfitters at Jan Thiel to make it a one-stop-shop sort of deal – a good choice if you're looking to dive without having to drive all over the island.

37 Revel in Colorful STREET ART

ART | CULTURAL COMMENTARY | WALKING

The bright colonial buildings along Punda's waterfront may be what catches your eye first, but the city's best art can be found on walls tucked in alleyways and along the storefronts of small businesses. Willemstad is positively covered in large murals depicting the unique environment and diverse community that calls Curaçao home – it's well worth seeking out these hidden treasures.

GEORG BERG/ALAMY MURAL ART BY BLENDCURACAO

How to

Getting here: To find street art in Willemstad, all you need to do is start walking! The greatest concentrations of murals can be found in Otrobanda and Scharloo.

When to go: Any time, all the time. You'll get the best photos on sunny days, though.

Tip: Most murals feature an artist signature, often with an Instagram account – look them up to see how else you can support their art!

MULEVICH/SHUTTERSTOCK

AJAK9511/SHUTTERSTOCK

Far left top Mural, Kaya Kaya Festival
Far left bottom Art souvenirs, Willemstad street market
Left Art on display, Willemstad

Like neighboring Aruba, Curaçao has fully embraced the positive impact that street art has on a city, and huge murals can be found all over Willemstad.

You'll find dozens of them in Otrobanda, largely thanks to the **Kaya Kaya Festival**. Headed up by Kurt Schoop, Raygen Zuiverloon and Clayton Lasten (Schoop and Lasten also run Bario Hotel and its restaurants), Kaya Kaya focuses on creating economic opportunities for the residents of Otrobanda through art, music and community projects. At past Kaya Kayas, artists have painted new murals, concerts and outdoor theaters have taken over the streets, and community members have implemented new neighborhood amenities like steps and playgrounds. If you're not in town for the festival or any other Kaya Kaya events, you can still partake in the art magic – the organization offers excellent street art tours every Thursday at 5:30pm for US$35 per person (bookable via kayakaya.org).

Across the river in Scharloo, **Street Art Skalo** (scharlooabou.com/street-art-skalo) is doing similar work, covering the former merchant neighborhood in colorful murals and sculptures – don't miss the gorgeous mural *3 O'Clock Romance* by artist Francis Sling. To see more of the art in Scharloo, Punda (and Otrobanda), book in with **Dushi Walks**; it also offers combo art/history walks and tours in English, Dutch, Papiamentu and Spanish.

Kaya Kaya Happenings

At the time of writing, Kaya Kaya announced that it will be changing its format from a week-long street festival to a year-round organization with frequent events in addition to the party in August.

As of now, Kaya Kaya hosts an Art Week in late May – where galleries pop up throughout the neighborhood, displaying local artists' work in technicolor settings – and a regularly occurring market supporting local entrepreneurs called **Amor Pa Otrobanda**. Shop for crafts, indulge in food and enjoy the live music floating through Otrabanda's streets.

Follow @kayakayafestival on Instagram for more details as the festival evolves into a full-fledged movement.

Listings

BEST OF THE REST

Party Spots

Emporio $$

A small nightclub and lounge for those who want to dance until the wee hours. Emporio hosts specialty parties throughout the week and has a solid happy-hour special.

Sunday Boat Parties $$$

Exactly what it sounds like: daytime revelers hit Fuik Bay every Sunday for an afternoon of partying in the sun. Several operators run boats out near Spaanse Water, with some including drinks and other BYOB. The crowd is young and the DJs are loud.

Best Cocktail Stops

BKLYN $$

With a chic aesthetic and thoughtful menu inspired by NYC but a heart that's all Caribbean, BKLYN serves up unique fusion cocktails that are somehow big city and tropical at the same time.

BijBlauw $$

This hotel restaurant/bar does more than just drinks, but it offers a sublime setting for happy hour that's hard to beat. Grab a spritz and let the sea breeze carry you away.

Caffeine Fixes

La Reina $

This beautiful cafe stuns with gorgeous tile work and a dreamy patio, and the food and drink vibe matches the energy – snag a butterfly pea latte or a smoothie and peruse the cute homeware shop inside.

James $

Tucked away in a Pietermaai alleyway, James feels like a hidden treasure. Organic, modern decor complements a filling breakfast menu, frothy lattes and fresh juices.

Van Gogh Specialty Coffee & City Roastery $

Housed in a robin's-egg-blue building in Pietermaai, Van Gogh is a drink emporium of sorts, serving up an impressively long list of hot coffees, 'super blend' lattes, specialty teas, kombucha and pressed juice.

Excellent Eats

Bliss the Berry $

A Mambo Beach lunch spot serving beautifully presented smoothies, açaí bowls, paninis, sandwiches and breakfast fare – don't miss the mile-high pancakes. It also serves coffee and bright brunch-oriented cocktails.

Komedor Kriyoyo $

Located out near Landhuis Bloemhof, Komedor does the Curaçao classics and does them well. Dig into one of its many stews: plantain, vegetable, cucumber, beef tongue and oxtail are all up for grabs.

Zest Restaurant and Beach Cafe $$

The Jan Thiel choice for somewhat elevated fare, Zest offers fun spritzes and a lengthy wine menu. Grab a seat at the beach bar for a meal under fairy lights and Caribbean stars.

Villa Vis Jan Thiel $$

This cheerful marina-side eatery in Caracasbaai specializes in fresh fish: take your pick from Caribbean sea bass, wahoo, grouper, tuna and more. Enjoy water views from the covered patio.

Bistro Botanika $$

Only open on Fridays and Saturdays, this local brunch favorite captures hearts with items like its pumpkin pancakes, carne asada burritos and fun cocktails like the frozen mango mint margarita.

Lemon Tree $$$

The restaurant of the Pietermaai's new Art Hotel specializes in 'casual fine dining,' serving a five- and seven-course tasting menu featuring modern takes on Curaçaoan cuisine. Book ahead.

Galleries & Gardens

Gallery Alma Blou

One of the oldest and largest galleries in Curaçao showcasing Caribbean artists. The museum switched ownership in 2024, but continues to showcase rotating collections.

Artcave Francis Sling

This studio in Scharloo features the exuberant work of Francis Sling, the talent behind the famous *3 O'Clock Romance* mural; follow Sling's Facebook (facebook.com/artcave francissling) for updates on public workshops.

Nena Sanchez Gallery

Stop into this delightful studio shop in Punda to take home a piece of artist Nena Sanchez' artwork, which features colorful tropical motifs and her signature blue ladies. You'll spot her murals and sculptures around Willemstad, too.

Yubi Kirindongo Sculpture Garden

Located near Curaçao's airport, this gallery/museum/sculpture garden is an immersive adventure into the creative mine of Yubi Kirindongo, who crafts fantastical sculptures from reclaimed metal, a statement against pollution and ecological destruction on the island.

HORIZONS WWP/ALAMY

Gallery Alma Blou

Get Active

Curaçao Mangrove Rif Park

This little Otrobanda gem, near the cruise port, is the only city park in central Willemstad. Its mangrove forest has been lovingly restored, and a boardwalk takes you through the trees. Some may balk at the price of entry (US$15), but the money goes to environmental preservation on the island.

Deep Dives

Dive Center Pietermaai

Part of Scuba Lodge in Pietermaai, this laid-back outfit offers dive courses, snorkeling tours and 'fun dives' for folks who already have their certs.

Fundiving Curaçao

This organized dive center in Jan Thiel offers courses, guided dives, boat trips, and PADI Bubble Maker classes for kids aged eight and up.

Jan Thiel Diving

This dive company offers standard dive courses as well as interesting PADI specialties like night diving, underwater naturalist and deep diver courses.

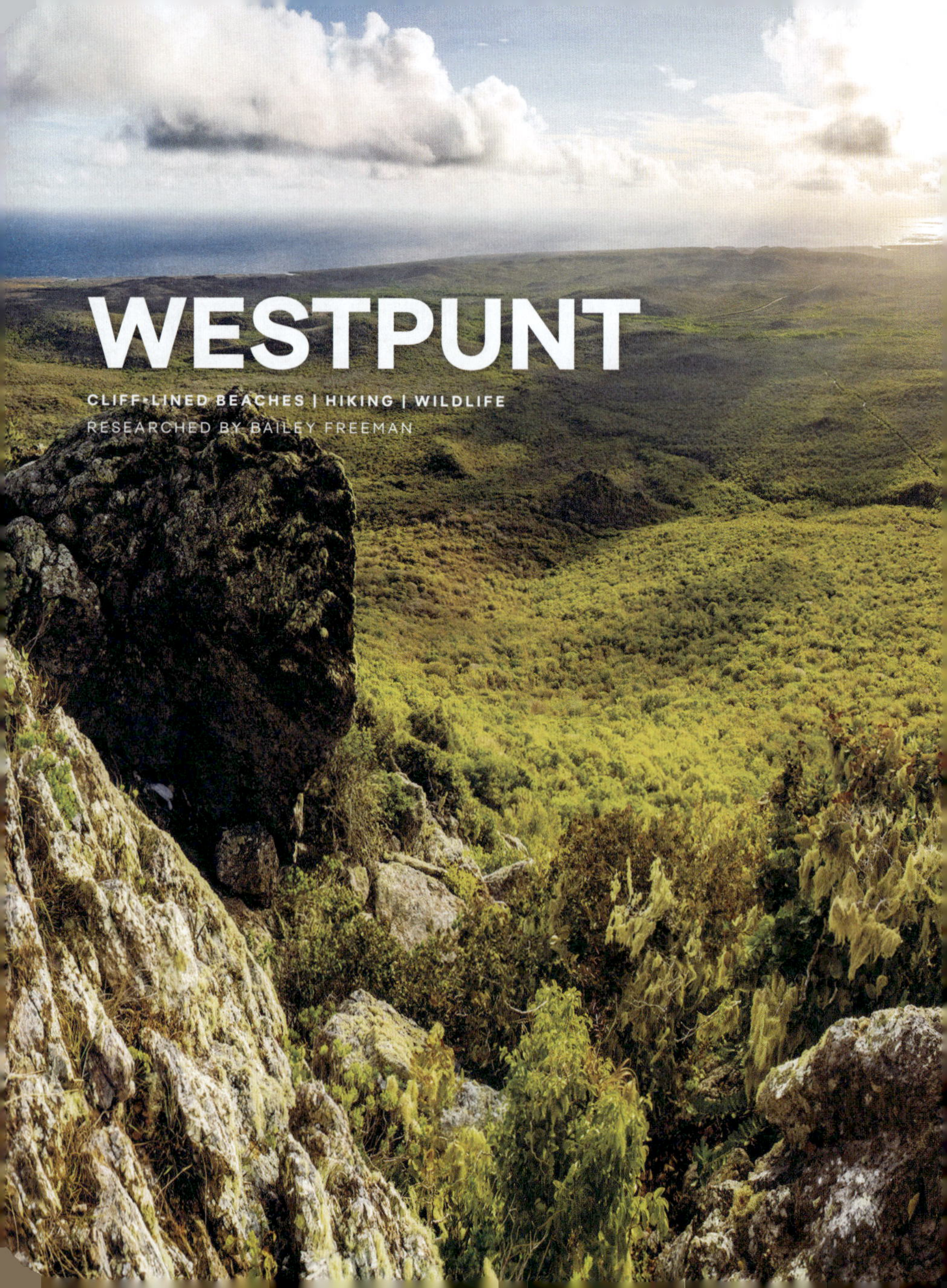

WESTPUNT

CLIFF-LINED BEACHES | HIKING | WILDLIFE

RESEARCHED BY BAILEY FREEMAN

WESTPUNT
Trip Builder

If Westpunt were a main dish, it'd be a fancy surf 'n' turf, baby. Curaçao's northern half delivers big on adventure on both land and sea – visit its national parks, lounge on its beaches or take to the waves.

FROM LEFT: Z JACOBS/SHUTTERSTOCK, Z JACOBS/SHUTTERSTOCK
PREVIOUS SPREAD: FREEDOM_WANTED/SHUTTERSTOCK

Practicalities

MONEY

There's one reliable ATM in Barber, but it only dispenses guilders and charges a steep transaction fee; get cash in Willemstad.

ARRIVING

Hato International Airport, Curaçao's airport on Willemstad's northwestern edge, is a good jumping-off point for exploring Westpunt without having to deal with traffic.

FIND YOUR WAY

Despite Westpunt's spread out, nature-forward vibe, getting around is a breeze. All the main roads are paved and maintained.

WHERE TO STAY

Westpunt features a handful of small villages, though few have much tourist infrastructure. A good option for lodging if you want a more remote experience.

Village	Pros/Cons
Sabana	Apartment rentals and small B&Bs. Few food options.
Sint Willibrordus	A handful of resorts. Few food options.

GETTING AROUND

Car and taxi A rental car allows you to hop between Westpunt's parks and beaches. Taxis don't generally run here. Either book a tour that includes transport or grab a rental.

On foot Apart from national park trails, Westpunt is not a walkable place. You have to drive to move from one village or beach to the next.

TOP: DIEGO VASQUEZ VILLASECA/SHUTTERSTOCK
BOTTOM: FOODSTCK/SHUTTERSTOCK

EATING & DRINKING

Westpunt isn't a culinary hub, but you'll find a few gems scattered around. Restaurants are mostly casual, serving international menus, sometimes with Dutch or Curaçaoan influence. You'll see your fair share of burgers and Mediterranean salads (pictured bottom left), but also a decent amount of fresh fish (pictured top left).

Best classic stewed beef Jaanchie's (p202)
Must-try goat burger Toko Williwood (p202)

ALL YEAR
You can visit Westpunt year-round, but there are some key events to catch.

MAY
The Seú Harvest Festival takes place in Hofi Abou, featuring a parade that marches down to Barber.

NOV
Dia di Willibrordus takes place in Seru Largu National Park, commemorating the area's history.

38 Great National PARKS

MOUNTAINS | BLOWHOLES | UNIQUE TRAILS

Looking northwest, the Willemstad sprawl gives way to Curaçao's wild side, a hilly, green expanse rimmed by rocky cliffs, pocket inlets and great beaches. A large section of Westpunt is occupied by the island's two national parks: Christoffel National Park and Shete Boka National Park. Each park delivers a different experience. Hit both to see the dynamic nature of Curaçao's outdoors.

How to

Getting here: You'll need a car; Christoffel is about 40 minutes from central Willemstad and Shete Boka is just five minutes further up the road.

When to go: Shete Boka's hours are 9am to 5pm, with last admittance at 4pm. Plan to get to Christoffel early, as the park has limited hours. More below.

Tip: Hit Christoffel in the morning and then head over to Shete Boka to cool off in the sea spray.

Centered around Mt Christoffel, **Christoffel National Park** encompasses the Savonet Plantation – formerly a large-scale agricultural and livestock plantation worked by hundreds of enslaved people – which has returned to a mostly untouched landscape teeming with wildlife: white-tailed deer, barn owls, hummingbirds, blaublau lizards and iguanas.

One of the best features of the park is its mountainside plant life, a florid mix of bromeliads, orchids and hanging lichen.

Accessing Christoffel takes a bit of planning, as the park closes at 2pm, with last admittance at 1:30pm (a measure taken to avoid heat-related injuries).

If you plan on making the hike up Mt Christoffel or driving the mountainside loop, the rangers require that you arrive prior to 10am. Entry is US$15.

TAMAS-V/GETTY IMAGES

Shete Boka National Park is the yang to Christoffel's yin, a dazzling stretch of coastline that puts the power of Curaçao's sea on full display. The name means 'Seven Mouths,' a reference to the park's yawning pocket inlets that funnel the waves into thunderous explosions of water; in reality, there are actually 10 inlets, all accessible by rustic trails across the rocky terrain.

The area is a protected nesting site for hawksbill, loggerhead and green turtles, with local researchers monitoring the area year-round. Shete Boka's hours are 9am to 5pm, with last admittance at 4pm, and entry is US$15.

Beat the Heat

Curaçao's national parks should feature prominently on any itinerary, but come prepared. The sun gets very hot, shade is rare in both parks, and natural water sources are not common, so heat-related issues should be guarded against.

The national park system advises that visitors bring two liters of water per person, as well as snacks for the trail. The UV index in Curaçao is extremely high, so good sunscreen, a hat and sunglasses are all essential gear as well; if you plan on hiking the mountain, wear good hiking shoes (not sandals).

Above Mt Christoffel

39 Take a Dip at the BEACHES

CORAL-STONE CLIFFS | UNDERWATER DELIGHTS | WHITE SAND

Chances are you're heading to Westpunt for beach time. Hemmed in by dramatic cliffs, Curaçao's beaches are fabulous getaways with cozy, intimate atmospheres. The beaches vary in size and amenities, ranging from rustic to fully kitted out. Most are within a 20-minute drive of each other, making beach-hopping a fun way to experience Curaçao's coast.

How to

Getting here: As with everything in Westpunt, you'll need a car. If you plan on beach-hopping, you can get to most with a low-clearance vehicle, but proceed with caution to Cas Abou.

When to go: Any time the sun is shining, which is most of the time in Curaçao.

Tip: Don't forget your snorkel gear! And pack snacks if you're headed to smaller beaches, as they may not have amenities.

Big & Little Beaches

Starting up north you'll find **Grote Knip** and **Kleine Knip**. 'Big' Knip is a family friendly pie-slice of sand and incandescent water with bathrooms, sun loungers and occasionally a food truck in the parking lot serving snacks and smoothies.

'Little' Knip doesn't have any facilities (however, new bathrooms were under construction at the time of research), but it does have some of the best snorkeling in Curaçao thanks to the colorful reefs wrapped around the base of its cliffs. Sometimes you'll find folks whipping up snacks at a food stand right on the beach.

Top Spot for Locals

South of the Knips sits **Playa Lagún**, a local favorite and another good spot to break out the snorkel gear. The beach itself is small but characterful thanks to a few wooden boats that have

FOKKE BAARSSEN/SHUTTERSTOCK

Revolutionary History

The Knip beaches are located on land that used to be part of the Kenepa Plantation, the site of Curaçao's largest uprising of enslaved people. Inspired by the Haitian Revolution, an enslaved man named Tula Rigaud amassed a resistance numbering 2000 – the total enslaved population on Curaçao at the time was 12,000 – and organized a monthlong revolt against the island's enslavers in August 1795. The uprising was ultimately quelled and Tula was executed two months later.

The event represents an important moment in Curaçao's history. August 17, the first day of the revolt, is recognized as a historic day in the long struggle for liberation.

taken up permanent residence on the sand. The only facilities here are pay-to-use bathrooms, but there is a restaurant up on the hill if you're hungry.

Closer to Town

The two beaches closest to Willemstad are **Cas Abou** (sometimes spelled Cas Abao) and **Playa Porto Mari**. The former is the Goldilocks of Curaçao beaches – not too big and not too small, home to a lovely sand/water combo and a restaurant to sustain you during your visit.

Playa Porto Mari takes amenities up a notch with a beach shop, showers, lockers and a more robust restaurant.

Above Cas Abou

40 Sint Willibrordus' FLAMINGOS

WILDLIFE | NATIONAL PARK | HISTORY

While Westpunt's coastline gets most of the shine, the south-central part of the region, an area known as Sint Willibrordus, is home to a fascinating scene worth exploring – the town and its surrounds are home to five different ecosystems, making it one of the most biodiverse places on the island. Hop onto one of the many trails or simply take in the flamingo-filled view.

OLIVER HOFFMANN/SHUTTERSTOCK

How to

Getting here: Sint Willibrordus is just north of Willemstad's outer reaches – you'll need a car to get there.

When to go: Go early in the morning or around sunset for the best experience; Curaçao's interior can turn sweltering at midday.

Tip: This area is also home to one of Curaçao's weirdest photo ops: the Williwood sign. Snap a picture and then head to Toko for burgers.

GAIL JOHNSON/SHUTTERSTOCK

MARLY DE KOK/SHUTTERSTOCK

Far left top Flamingos, Curaçao
Far left bottom Sint Willibrordus Church
Left Cactuses, near Sint Willibrordus

The hamlet of Sint Willibrordus is not much of a destination in and of itself, but it's perched on the edge of one of Curaçao's most biodiverse areas: Rif Sint Marie and Hermanus Nature Reserve. Made up of two former salt plantations, these natural areas encompass a whopping five different ecosystems – a rather impressive feat that's earned it a Ramsar designation.

Within their borders sit one of the most well-preserved bits of reef in the Caribbean, a seagrass ecosystem, the saltwater lake home to Curaçao's famous flamingos, mangroves and dry tropical forest. The reserves were recently united under one umbrella and are now part of **Seru Largu National Park**, Curaçao's newest national park.

Start off by visiting the **flamingo observation point** on the northeast side of the lake – while flamingo numbers can vary, you'll very likely spot at least a few prancing through the waters. Note: flamingos are easily stressed, so don't go chasing any birds.

Then hit one of the area's three main trails: the **Seru Largu Hiking Trail**, the **Coastal Trail** and the **Plains Trail**. The park also hosts several guided tours (and some can be booked upon request for groups). Join a guide for a morning hike to the coast, or stay after dark for a full-moon hike. Tours run between US$8 and US$10 per person; find booking info on the park website (serulargupark.org) and ping the listed email for any park-related queries. They answer quickly!

Project Salu

The Seru Largu's controlling entity **Carmabi** (Caribbean Research and Management of Biodiversity) is currently working on what it calls Project Salu, a cultural history initiative highlighting the area's role as a salt plantation. The goal of this project is to highlight the area's history and the role slavery played in its development.

Volunteers are constructing lime kilns and a mini salt pan for educational purposes, and future programming is aimed at bringing in both community members and tourists.

Contact the park (serulargupark.org) to learn more.

Listings

BEST OF THE REST

Local Noshes

Jaanchie's $

This iconic Westpunt stop near Sabana has been serving Curaçaoan favorites since 1936. Walk through the flower-covered walkway, take a seat on the breezy patio and dive into heaped servings of goat or iguana stew. Don't miss the fresh juices, especially the oregano punch.

Restaurant Playa Forti $$

Perched on the cliff overlooking Playa Forti, dining here feels like eating on an island in the sky overlooking nothing but blue ocean. Dive into a whole red snapper or a seafood pasta while daredevils cliff jump and the sun sinks below the horizon.

Bahia Restaurant $$

The closest food stop to little Playa Lagún, Bahia specializes in casual international fare, but the real draw is the view over the beach and the occasional iguana visitor (don't worry, they're polite).

Toko Williwood $$

One of the few food options in the Sint Willibrordus area, Toko Williwood is a good place to snag a burger (even a goat one!). Stop by on Sundays for its weekend barbecue, too.

Isabelle off the Beach $$

Located halfway between Shete Boka and the Sabana beach community, this spot serves an eclectic international menu in chic, sunny surrounds. Only open Thursday through Sunday.

Coffee & Beer

Island Breeze Coffee $

This adorable little coffee truck on the east side of Willibrordus makes for a refreshing pit stop – grab some caffeine or one of its luxurious smoothies (helloooo banana/passion fruit). Take it to go or enjoy your drink on the cute little patio.

Japie's $

In a land of tropical cocktails and sangria, Japie's stands out as a true beerhouse – grab a small-batch fruit beer, tripel or blonde and settle into the sports-bar-esque dining area just northwest of Barber for a laid-back afternoon.

More Amazing Westpunt Beaches

Playa Kalki

One of Westpunt's most northerly beaches (just north of Sabana), Playa Kalki offers a pier, roped-off swimming area, *cabañas* for rent and a beach restaurant with restrooms.

FOKKE BAARSSEN/SHUTTERSTOCK

Playa Kalki

It can get crowded on the weekends, so avoid peak time for the best experience.

Playa Grandi

This Sabana beach is a favorite for visitors, especially families, thanks to its numerous resident turtles. That said, if you visit, treat the turtles with respect and keep your distance.

Playa Forti

This small rocky beach south of Playa Grandi is a nice option if you're looking for a quiet waterside spot to escape the masses. The current is a bit strong, so you should be a strong swimmer if you hit the water; Forti is best known as a good place for cliff jumping into the water.

Playa Jeremi

This local favorite near Lagún is cozily tucked away from the bustle of the busier beaches. There are no services besides a few loungers, but there's some shade and good snorkeling along the cliffsides.

Other Westpunt Landmarks

Watamula Hole

Coastal erosion has created this almost perfectly round blowhole near the northernmost tip of the island – stick around to catch an explosion of water. Take care driving here, as the road leading to it is bumpy and unpaved.

Santa Martha Bay Viewpoint

The observation deck at Santa Martha Bay delivers sweeping views of the irregularly shaped bay and nearby Seru Largu. A worthwhile photo op if you're in the area.

JOKE VAN EEGHEM/SHUTTERSTOCK

Santa Martha Bay

Get Active

Marijke's Nature Trail

This privately managed trail system winds through the hills, lagoons and coastline near Soto and can be done independently, but we recommend taking a guided tour to get the most out of your experience (marijkesnaturetrail.com); the organization offers moonlight hikes and also 'wet hikes' through the water, and can organize campfire and barbecue hikes, too.

E-Nature Curaçao

Want to explore inland Curaçao without having to hike it? Book a tour with E-Nature and take to the trails on its signature e-buggies. The three-hour tour takes you through the St Michel area and covers the area's history and nature.

Rent Adventure Curaçao

Based out of Grote Knip, this outfitter provides some nice rental options to maximize your time at the beach, including snorkel gear, stand-up paddleboards and sea scooters.

Practicalities

Right Eagle Beach (p66), Aruba

EASY STEPS FROM THE AIRPORT TO THE CITY CENTER

Most people's gateway to the ABCs will be through Aruba, as the Queen Beatrix Airport (pictured below) is the biggest and fields flights from the most international cities. It is possible to fly straight to Curaçao and Bonaire, but connecting cities are more limited. Flights between the islands are frequent, allowing for maximum flexibility.

AT THE AIRPORT

SIM CARDS

It's possible to buy SIM cards at airports across the islands, but like everything at the airport, they'll be more expensive. Snag one from supermarkets or local cell shops. The main network providers are Digicel (all islands), Setar (Aruba) and Flow (Bonaire and Curaçao).

CURRENCY EXCHANGE

Each airport offers exchange services, but it's generally recommended to wait and exchange currency at local banks for better rates. US dollars are accepted everywhere alongside local currencies, but you'll probably want to swap euros for something else.

EQROY/SHUTTERSTOCK

Wi-fi Airports have wi-fi, but signal strength varies. Curaçao offers free wi-fi with an hour 'limit,' but you can reconnect once the limit is reached.

ATMs Each airport has ATMs – grab cash if you plan on snagging a taxi or bus to your destination; not all taxis take cards.

Charging Queen Beatrix has no charging stations, only rare outlets. Bonaire has stations in its 'Rest Zones.' Hato has stations in its terminals and Arrivals Hall.

ENTRY PROTOCOL

Aruba Visitors must complete the registration for an ED card (edcardaruba.aw) within a week prior to arrival. Cost US$20.

Bonaire Visitors must pay an entry tax of US$75 (tourismtax.bonairegov.com). Pay in advance or at the airport.

Curaçao Visitors must complete registration for a free immigration card (dicardcuracao.com/dicard).

GETTING TO THE CITY CENTERS

CAR All islands have rental-car services at their airports; parking is easy and often free in Willemstad and Kralendijk, even in the most central areas. Most parking in central Oranjestad is paid, but the rates are reasonable; enforcement is strict, however.

BUS Aruba and Curaçao have bus services from the airport available, but this won't be the best choice if you have a lot of luggage (some buses may not even let you on). That said, this is the most budget-friendly option by a long shot.

TAXI The most expensive choice for leaving the airport, but sometimes the only option, particularly in Bonaire. Taxi rates in Aruba are standardized, while rates in Curaçao vary by company.

ARUBA Taxis downtown or to the resort areas cost US$20 to US$30. An Arubus line passes near the airport, but luggage larger than a carry-on is not permitted.

BONAIRE Taxis go to downtown Kralendijk for around US$20. There are no public-transportation options.

CURAÇAO Taxis to downtown Willemstad cost between US$40 and US$60 – ouch. Buses run from the airport to Punda and Otrobanda for a couple of guilders, but they don't stop at any accommodations. Follow the bus system schedule using its app (ABC Curaçao).

OTHER POINTS OF ENTRY

Oranjestad, Kralendijk and Willemstad are the only points of entry for Aruba, Bonaire and Curaçao respectively, both for flights and cruises (all cruise terminals are in the cities' central harbors). Aruba fields the most international connections besides Bonaire and Curaçao, mostly from the US (Boston, Miami, Washington DC, Atlanta, among several others), plus flights from Canada (Toronto), the Caribbean (Santo Domingo, Sint Maarten) and South America (Bogotá, Lima, Paramaribo, São Paolo). The only European flights come from Amsterdam.

Curaçao comes in second variety-wise, with the majority of its flights arriving from the Caribbean (Santo Domingo, Punta Cana, Sint Maarten, Port of Spain), and Central and South America (Caracas, Belo Horizonte, Panama City, Barranquilla, Bogotá, Medellín). There are some flights from the US (New York, Miami, Charlotte, Atlanta) and Canada (Toronto, Montreal), and like Aruba, the only European connection is Amsterdam. Bonaire's tiny airport mainly fields flights from Aruba and Curaçao. Some US flights connect (New York, Miami, Atlanta, Houston); the only direct Caribbean flights come from Sint Maarten and Santo Domingo, the only Canadian flights from Toronto, the only South American flights from Barranquilla, and the only European flights from Amsterdam.

TRANSPORT TIPS TO HELP YOU GET AROUND

Due to their small size and relatively flat terrain, the ABCs are a cinch to navigate. While some public-transportation options do exist, having a car of your own will make your time much more enjoyable – less time waiting around, more time exploring.

CAR RENTALS

Options abound for car rentals; many international companies are represented, as well as some small local ones (particularly in Aruba). Always make reservations well in advance, particularly in high season. Check your policies to make sure any intended destinations are not prohibited.

PUBLIC BUSES

Public transportation exists on Aruba and Curaçao, but not Bonaire. In Aruba, Arubus (arubus.com) connects most major tourist areas, beaches and hotels. Curaçao's bus system (autobusbedrijf.com) is decent for getting around Willemstad and connecting to Mambo Beach/Jan Thiel, but wait times can be long.

CAR RENTAL PER DAY

Sub-compact	US$50–60
Van	US$90–100
4WD	US$80–90

NO CELL PHONES Across the ABCs it's illegal to use cell phones while driving. Hands-free set-ups are OK – we suggest investing in a phoneholder before you arrive – but texting (and even mapping your journey) could land you in hot water and earn you a hefty fine.

DRIVING ESSENTIALS

Drive on the right side of the road; car steering wheels are on the left.

One-way streets are common in city centers; the ring road in Bonaire also becomes a one-way north of the Hato neighborhood heading toward Gotomeer.

Right turns on red are prohibited in the ABCs.

Skip driving at night in more rural areas, if you can – they aren't well lit.

Give way to the right at intersections.

GO SLOW Speed limits across the islands are relatively slow compared to US and European highway speed limits – 40km/h (25mph) in town, only up to 80km/h (50mph) on big roads. Take your time and resist the urge to put the pedal to the metal, even on empty roads. It's not uncommon for wildlife to cross in rural areas – from giant iguanas to donkeys – and slower speeds keep everyone safe.

CYCLE WITH CARE

While cycling is not impossible, anyone planning to travel their island of choice on two wheels should keep their head on a swivel. Bike lanes aren't common and many of the larger roads don't have shoulders.

ROAD CONDITIONS

Main roads in Aruba are in decent shape, but things get bumpy quickly when you turn off them, sometimes even in urban neighborhoods. Bonaire's roads are sealed but can sometimes get patchy in rural spots after rain; the road to Lac Cai is unpaved. Curaçao has good, sealed roads on the majority of the island, though potholes do appear.

INSURANCE

Insurance policies for car rentals are standard; that said, it's always good to have additional insurance beyond your normal car insurance to cover any damages, either with a credit card or other mode of travel insurance.

BOAT TRANSPORTATION

Transportation by sea isn't common unless you're heading out on an excursion; the only exceptions are the water taxis that go to Klein Bonaire from Kralendijk and to Renaissance Island from Oranjestad (pictured below).

KNOW YOUR CARBON FOOTPRINT

A one-way flight from Aruba to Curaçao would emit roughly 34kg of carbon dioxide per passenger; that amount goes up to 50kg per passenger if going to Bonaire.

These numbers come from the International Civil Aviation Organization; check out its website *(icao.int)* and calculate your own journey.

ILDI PAPP/SHUTTERSTOCK

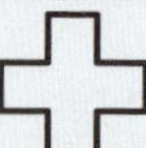

SAFE TRAVEL

The ABCs are generally safe, welcoming places with some of the lowest crime rates in the Caribbean; that said, a common-sense approach to travel always applies. Be vigilant and you'll have a grand time exploring.

WATCH YOUR BELONGINGS Avoid leaving anything of value in your car when you go snorkeling, diving or hiking – petty thievery can happen. Locals tend to leave their cars unlocked to avoid any busted windows, but it's generally best practice to just make sure nothing is in view, or to bring things with you.

HEAT EXHAUSTION The heat in the ABCs is sneaky thanks to the cover of the trade winds, but it can still get you thanks to the islands' proximity to the equator. Stay hydrated and reapply sunscreen frequently.

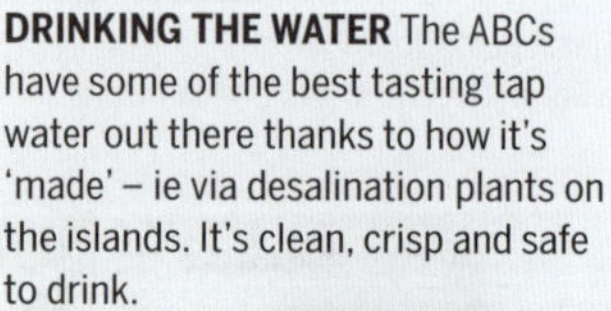

DRINKING THE WATER The ABCs have some of the best tasting tap water out there thanks to how it's 'made' – ie via desalination plants on the islands. It's clean, crisp and safe to drink.

MARIAN WEYO/SHUTTERSTOCK

OLIVER HOFFMANN/SHUTTERSTOCK

CAUTION ON THE EAST SIDE Each island's east coast is much rougher than its west thanks to the wind direction, and all caution signs regarding entering the water should be taken very seriously. Currents are strong and dangerous here.

BITES & STINGS

The islands are indeed tropical, which means mosquito-borne illnesses can be a thing (dengue, Zika, chikungunya). Dawn and dusk are the most active times for bites, so layer up on repellent, particularly if you're inland.

QUICK TIPS TO HELP YOU MANAGE YOUR MONEY

CREDIT CARDS

Credit cards are largely accepted across the islands, particularly in tourist areas. If you're headed to rural outposts, though, bring cash just in case.

BUDGET FOR FEES

This is particularly the case for Bonaire, which charges the standard visitors tax (US$75 for foreigners) and, for snorkelers, divers and hikers, the STINAPA nature fee (US$40). Rangers do check.

TIPPING

Where there's no service charge, it's normal to tip 15% to 20% of a restaurant bill. Guides also appreciate tips; it's usually US$5 to US$10 per dive tank, and US$10 per day for tour guides.

CURRENCY

US Dollar

HOW MUCH FOR A...

Beach club *cabaña*
US$8

Amstel Bright
US$5

Dinner for two at a modern restaurant
US$80

FINDING AN ATM

The majority of ATMs are concentrated in the capital cities, with the exception of Aruba's resort area. They generally dispense local currency, but you may find some that distribute US dollars. Some more rural ATMs only accept local debit cards, so plan ahead if you're venturing beyond city limits.

ARUBA, BONAIRE & CURAÇAO

The ABC islands are well-connected money-wise with the rest of the world and transactions are generally quick and easy, but there are differences between islands. Aruba uses the florin (AWG), Curaçao uses the Caribbean guilder (Cg) and Bonaire uses the US dollar. US dollars are accepted across the islands, but you can't use the florin in Curaçao or the guilder in Aruba.

PAYING FOR GAS

Not all gas stations accept credit and debit cards – some are cash only, others only accept local debit cards. Bring cash, just in case.

SKIP THE HAGGLING

Haggling is not very common in the ABCs, so it's best to just move on if an item is too expensive.

VISITING ON A BUDGET

Aruba, Bonaire and Curaçao aren't exactly budget destinations, but they also aren't priced sky-high. Budget accommodations like hostels do exist, particularly in Aruba and Curaçao, and it's easy to self-cater if you're looking to cut food costs (but remember to bring your own bags to the grocery store). PADI lists Bonaire in its three cheapest places to dive in the Caribbean – a win for underwater explorers – citing dive resorts as good package deals.

RESPONSIBLE TRAVEL

ON THE ROAD

Bring your own bags. Grocery stores have eliminated plastic bags, so unless you want to carry everything in your arms, bring a reusable one.

Watch your water. Water is not an easily replenished resource on these islands, so be mindful of your usage.

Skip animal encounters. Don't book with operators that promise animal interactions or touch experiences.

Don't step on the coral. One of the biggest rules of the ABCs – do not touch!

Wash your gear. Sanitize your gear between snorkels and dives to avoid spreading contaminants from site to site.

Pack out your beach day. Don't leave anything behind in the sand, especially smaller items like wrappers and cigarette butts.

Leave the shells. Don't take shells from the beach. At best it's bad for the environment; at worst it's illegal.

NATUREPICS_LI/GETTY IMAGES

GIVE BACK

Reef Renewal International works with environmental and park entities in Curaçao (pictured above) and Bonaire to research and restore damaged reefs.

Get certified to do reef restoration and help local entities plant new corals. Book Reef Restoration Dives at several dive outfits.

Volunteer with Sea Turtle Conservation Bonaire projects aimed at preserving sea turtles' environments: beach clean-ups, in-water surveys, nesting site protection, fishing-line clean-ups and more.

Volunteer to help restore Aruba's biodiversity and protect it from climate change through tree-planting initiatives organized by Ban Lanta y Planta.

Donate to Aruba and Bonaire's donkey sanctuaries (Bonaire sanctuary pictured right), or if you're staying on the islands longer, consider volunteering.

DOS & DON'TS

Do observe wildlife at safe distances.

Don't try to take advantage of discounts for locals.

Do opt for reef-safe sunscreens without oxybenzone.

Don't party too hard on the beach. Vacations are for letting loose, but not in a way that disrupts the environment around you.

LEAVE A SMALL FOOTPRINT

Plastic waste is a huge problem for small Caribbean islands, as evidenced by the immense amount of microplastics that the current washes up on their eastern shores; it's worth noting that much of this pollution comes from larger landmasses, not the ABCs themselves. In fact, single-use plastics are banned in Aruba and Bonaire. Do as the locals do and reduce plastic consumption on the islands, skipping disposable water bottles and other small plastics whenever possible.

TMGENZO/SHUTTERSTOCK

SUPPORT LOCAL

Buy smart and skip mass-produced tchotchkes for artist-made work, often available at local hotels and galleries.

Book local by researching your choice of accommodations and seeing if they are foreign-owned. Best practice is to support local hoteliers.

Venture out – even if you book at an all-inclusive, make a point of going off-grounds to support nearby businesses.

CLIMATE CHANGE & TRAVEL

Lonely Planet urges all travelers to engage with their travel carbon footprint, which will mainly come from air travel. While there often isn't an alternative, travelers can look to minimize the number of flights they take, opt for newer aircrafts and use cleaner ground transport, such as trains.

One proposed solution – purchasing carbon offsets – unfortunately does not cancel out the impact of individual flights. While most destinations will depend on air travel for the foreseeable future, for now, pursuing ground-based travel where possible is the best course of action.

The UN Carbon Offset Calculator shows how flying impacts a household's emissions:

The ICAO's carbon emissions calculator allows visitors to analyse the CO2 generated by point-to-point journeys:

RESOURCES

greenglobe.com

acf.aw

stinapabonaire.org

carmabi.org

ACCOMMODATIONS

Accommodations options run the gamut from luxe resorts to midrange apartments to backpacker-centric hostels. The only thing you won't find on these islands is camping options. But if you're looking for signature accommodations, book into a dive resort for a truly immersive experience (see what we did there?).

FOKKE BAARSSEN/SHUTTERSTOCK

ALL-INCLUSIVES

Ah, the classic Caribbean all-inclusive. These sprawling resorts offer everything on-site, which is a boon for families or folks with limited vacation time who just want to relax.

You'll find more of these options in Aruba and Curaçao than in Bonaire, and they vary in format: some are large-scale high-rises, while others are smaller and almost boutique-like, with interesting features like swim-up rooms, wellness-retreat facilities and more.

All-inclusive prices are higher in Aruba than in Curaçao.

BOUTIQUE HOTELS

Trendy boutique hotels offer some of the hippest options across the islands – stay in mural-covered bungalows, lounge in hammocks on breezy patios or take a post-sun nap in UNESCO-certified buildings for atmospheric stays. Prices vary based on proximity to attractions and amenities, but there's usually a midrange option available.

APARTMENTS

Apartment rentals are a great option for families and groups who desire more privacy and want to self-cater. Many small complexes around the islands rent out condos with kitchens and balconies, and some even have monthly rates if you're looking to stay for a longer period of time.

BYVALET/SHUTTERSTOCK

FOCUSED ADVENTURES/SHUTTERSTOCK

DIVE RESORTS

The ABCs offer excellent diving opportunities, and dive resorts built around the experience make hitting the water almost unfathomably easy. Some resorts offer their services in packages, where you can choose to just book rooms, book rooms and dives together, or book rooms and certification courses together. Others offer services as à la carte options you can add to the overall booking, skipping packages for customized experiences that vary by day. These resorts also provide transport to dive sites (including offshore ones), allowing you to skip the car rental if you're just looking to dive during your vacation, not a bad money saving hack.

Because they have everything easily on hand, dive resorts are a great place to complete your certifications, the most common of which being PADI or SSI. Finish the e-learning portion of your course before you arrive; once you're there, the open-water dive portion of the certification can be done over three days. If you want to spend less of your vacation studying and completing practicum, you can begin your certification process at home and complete what's called a 'referral course' once you arrive; this only takes a day and a half, allowing you to use the rest of the time to dive at will.

BOOKING

While it may be possible to book accommodations when you arrive, we don't recommend it. Booking ahead ensures you'll be covered, and you should book way ahead for peak season (December to March), as the islands fill up with cold folks from the northern hemisphere and Carnival revelers.

The most common booking sites for these islands are the big ones – Google, Expedia, Booking.com, etc – but you may score a better deal if you book directly through a hotel website.

Aruba Tourism Board (aruba.com) Features a comprehensive list of accommodations and lets you filter by interest, hotel type and nearby beaches.

My Curaçao Guide (mycuracaoguide.com) Local publication with a list of accommodations where you can search by amenities and neighborhoods.

Bonaire Tourism Board (bonaireisland.com) Lets you peruse the island's hotels and filter by 'blue-certified,' ie verified as sustainable for marine environments.

EVERYONEPHOTO STUDIO/SHUTTERSTOCK

HOSTELS

While the ABCs definitely cater more to mid- and high-range accommodations, hostels still exist! You'll find the cheapest beds in Bonaire and the most expensive in Aruba.

ESSENTIAL NUTS & BOLTS

KEEP BEACHWEAR AT THE BEACH

While it's tempting to roll into nearby restaurants in a swimsuit, it's frowned upon and some places may not let you enter.

SKIP THE GLASS

Glass containers in beach and pool areas pose a serious injury hazard if they break. Leave the bottles in the hotel room.

BEACH BATHROOMS

Many beaches don't have bathrooms – have a potty plan that doesn't disturb the ecosystem (WAG bags are a great option!).

FAST FACTS

Time Zone
GMT-4

Aruba Country Code
+297

Electricity
127V/60Hz

GOOD TO KNOW

Visa requirements vary between the ABCs, but citizens of most countries do not need a visa to enter.

The legal drinking age is 18 years old.

Vegan and vegetarian options have increased significantly in recent years.

Etiquette across the islands generally mirrors that of South America and is relatively laid-back. Just be nice!

Shop and restaurant closures on Sundays are common; plan ahead for meals and other immediate needs.

ACCESSIBLE TRAVEL

The Aruba tourism board website (aruba.com/us/our-island/island-facts/special-needs) has a list of accessible hotels, as well as accessibility services on the island.

Large hotels generally offer accessible rooms, but inquire about specific needs. Dolphin Suites in Curaçao is a fully accessible hotel, including its beach.

Beaches vary in accessibility; some have steps, and others are flat but no wheelchair ramps. Aruba has the most accessible beaches of the islands and Palm Beach has accessible *palapas* (palm-covered shelters).

Restaurant accessibility is mixed, with the historic centers generally presenting the most issues. New constructions have more reliable accessibility measures in place.

Diving operator Curious2Dive (curious2dive.com/en/diving-with-a-disability) in Curaçao offers accessible dive experiences, as do some dive resorts on the other islands.

Transport Aruba's Arubus has wheelchair ramps and designated areas.

COVER UP

While the ABCs are not conservative when it comes to beachwear, topless nudity is not allowed.

DON'T TOUCH THE TREES

Beach trees aren't meant for hammocks; in Aruba, some of them are considered national landmarks.

ISLAND TIME

It's a real thing – be patient, as everything moves at a relaxed pace in these parts.

FAMILY TRAVEL

Overall, the ABCs are family-friendly destinations. Bonaire may be better for older kids who can take advantage of all the water activities.

One Happy Family Aruba's tourism board has partnered with some local hotels and outfitters to offer family discounts.

Car seats Many car-rental companies offer car-seat rentals if you don't want to bring one from home.

Diving PADI offers 'Bubblemaker' courses for kids ages eight to 10. Inquire at dive shops.

SAY HELLO

Always greet and say goodbye to folks when in close quarters – bonus points if you do it in Papiamento. 'Bon dia,' 'Bon tardi' and 'Bon nochi' are all good standards to use, and locals will appreciate the effort.

DON'T DO DRUGS

Despite Dutch connections, the ABC islands have rather strict drug laws. Medical and recreational cannabis is illegal in Aruba, Bonaire and Curaçao, and penalties can be fairly severe if you're caught with it in hand. Our advice is to skip the risk.

SVET FOTO/SHUTTERSTOCK

LGBTIQ+ TRAVELERS

Marriage Same-sex marriage is legal on all three islands, and overall attitudes are welcoming. The general vibe is live-and-let-live.

Pride Aruba holds a Pride celebration in June, and Bonaire hosts a smaller affair that month as well; Curaçao holds its large Pride celebration in late September.

Going Out If you're looking for nightlife, both Curaçao and Aruba have one dedicated LGBTIQ+ nightclub each (Gaze and Cage, respectively), while other bars are considered queer-friendly.

For latest news, follow: @arubagayguide, @curacaopride.

Index

000 Map pages

000 Map pages

J

K

L

M

N

'That time two sweet folks from Bonaire offered to give me a tour of the entire island on their day off – and it was a wonderful day indeed.'

BAILEY FREEMAN

'That time I saw cave drawings hundreds of years old that told time by the stars and realized how amazing humans have always been.'

BAILEY FREEMAN

'The time I wasn't sure the sedan we rented would make it down the rocky roads of Arikok.'

ROBERT ISENBERG

TOP TO BOTTOM: STEPHANKOGELMAN/SHUTTERSTOCK, NORMA COELHO/SHUTTERSTOCK, LIESL VANDEPAEPELIERE/SHUTTERSTOCK

THIS BOOK

Destination Editor
James Smart

Production Editor
Sarah Farrell

Cartographer
Mark Griffiths

Image Editor
Dorota Michalec

Coordinating Editor
Simon Williamson

Cover Researcher
Giada De Agostinis

Thanks
Sofie Andersen, James Appleton, Michelle Bennett, Melanie Dankel, Alex Howard, Alicia Johnson, Kellie Langdon, Maura Murphy, Cliff Wilkinson